LEARNING THROUGH PLAY

# Music

LAUREL PEGG

**Published by Scholastic Ltd,**
Villiers House,
Clarendon Avenue,
Leamington Spa,
Warwickshire CV32 5PR
Text © Laurel Pegg
© 1998  Scholastic Ltd
1 2 3 4 5 6 7 8 9 0   8 9 0 1 2 3 4 5 6 7

**Author**
Laurel Pegg

**Editor**
Jane Bishop

**Assistant Editor**
Clare Miller

**Series designer**
Lynne Joesbury

**Designer**
Sarah Rock

**Illustrations**
Cathy Hughes

**Cover photograph**
© Digital Vision

Designed using Adobe Pagemaker

British Library Cataloguing-in-Publication Data
A catalogue record for this book is available from the British Library.

ISBN 0-590-53790-3

# CONTENTS

## Music in the nursery curriculum

Music can provide a valuable means of acquiring skills, knowledge and understanding within a holistic framework, utilizing all of the learning sites within the nursery setting such as the water, sand, home and construction areas. It can help to meet the objectives of the six areas of learning in SCAA/QCA's *Desirable Outcomes For Children's Learning* and plays a particularly important part in meeting the needs of the Creative Development area.

Many skills are used, for example, responding to cues, sharing and taking turns are all essential for playing music. Sorting, matching and sequencing are fundamental processes in creating and composing music, while listening carefully and observing are necessary for listening and responding to music.

Music learning does not depend on instrumental skills or understanding of music notation but rather on an involvement in the world of sound by making, playing, listening or responding to it. One of the first stages in music learning is to explore many different sound sources. Children listen, respond to, and play with, vocal and body sounds, the sounds of natural and made objects, and acoustic and electronic instruments. The unique contribution of music and the world of sound also helps children to make sense of their own inner, imaginative world; the expressive world of feelings and emotions.

## Resources

Music is often a learning area within the nursery which is under resourced. Yet it is a discrete subject in its own right, a major constituent of creative development and, as this book shows, able to facilitate learning in all of the other Desirable Outcome learning areas.

Sound sources, materials, toys and equipment found within the nursery can be used to achieve many of the activities described here. However, you will also need to provide a range of suitable acoustic and electronic instruments. Small instruments are not necessarily the easiest to manipulate for young children (finger cymbals and triangles for example) so choose ones which are feasible for the children to manipulate and control as well as providing good sound quality.

A good selection for the nursery would include: small whicker maracas, wooden claves, agogo and guiro, metal agogo, metal guiro, bell rings and sticks, tambourines, tambour, drums, cymbal, chime bars and a few larger instruments if space and finance permit (alto xylophone or metallophone and an electronic keyboard).

It is essential to have access to a tape recorder or CD player (choose a substantial model with large switches and a microphone input). Provide a bank of blank tapes for the children to record on to and a supply of recorded tapes for them to listen to. A small portable tape recorder with inbuilt microphone would be useful for collecting environmental sounds. Many stories and poems already in use in the nursery are useful stimuli to creative work and many of the CD Rom stories and story boards have sound sources included in them. Collect songs and rhymes onto tape and practise them so that you have them as a teacher-resource available to use within both planned and unplanned activities.

## Processes in music

All activities within music will involve children in one or all of the following at any given time. They should not be seen as separate but rather as interrelated processes. For example, it is impossible to perform, play or create music without listening attentively as well.

### Composing

Children are involved in emergent composition when they make, choose, reject, match, and sort sounds. When they make up musical sandwiches or music for fireworks or monsters they are creating, putting the sounds together for themselves and beginning to compose.

### Performing

Children are performing when they are playing instruments and sound sources or when they are singing and making vocal sounds. Emergent performance in the nursery covers a range of contexts. A child exploring freely in the sound area, playing a sound on an instrument being passed around a circle of children, singing a song or controlling a beat on a drum is beginning to learn performance skills.

### Listening

Children listen to a wide variety of sounds both within and outside the nursery. These will include body and vocal sounds such as clapping or humming, child-made sound sources, acoustic classroom instruments, electronic sources and a range of recorded music. Children should be encouraged to enter, explore and symbolize their own imaginative worlds through listening.

## The elements in music

Music is comprised of a number of different elements which interrelate to form a whole. All nursery children will naturally be involved in the elements through musical play, exploration and listening and should be encouraged to respond imaginatively to them.

### Timbre

Timbre refers to the individual sound quality of each instrument or voice; the specific sound of a wood block or a drum or a tambourine. This is the key element at nursery level and children will delight in exploring as many different sound sources as possible.

### Texture

Texture is used to describe one instrument or voice playing alone or many instruments playing together. Children can experience a sparse texture when they play a tambourine alone and a denser texture when a group of children play three or four instruments together.

### Dynamics

This element refers to the volume of sound, whether the piece of music is loud or quiet. Children can listen to loud and quiet music, move around to it in different ways, sing a favourite song loudly and quietly or make loud and quiet sounds.

### Tempo

Tempo describes the speed of a piece of music. Children can make, create and listen to fast and slow music, responding in different ways such as by moving around at fast and slow speeds.

### Pitch

Pitch is an extremely difficult concept for young children to grasp because they are already learning about high and low in relation to space. In music it refers to high and low sounds or 'frequencies'. Children should be encouraged to explore, make, listen and respond to high and low sounds without necessarily focusing on their understanding of the differences.

### Duration

Duration describes the length of a sound, whether it is short or long. Children can listen to long and short sounds and explore making long and short sounds in the sound area. Rhythm is made up of long and short sounds put together into patterns. Children will naturally copy rhythms which they have heard and will make up their own patterns.

### Structure

All or some of the elements will be combined in a piece of music to give it an overall structure. Understanding of the concepts 'same', 'not the same' and 'different' allows children to be involved in repetition and contrast. Within the nursery, children can copy a sound, make a different sound and progress, for instance, towards making musical sandwiches.

## Storage

A trolley with crates is useful for storing the smaller instruments. Ensure that wooden instruments and metal instruments are kept separately. Do not stand instruments on top of each other and store tambourines with the skin/plastic side adjacent. Keep beaters flat and away from the other instruments.

## Setting up the environment

Set up music as part of the whole environment within the nursery, where the children can explore, see and hear their own musical creations and symbols. You should aim to build up a cassette bank of recorded music, putting out one or two examples each week, perhaps with headphones.

Set up a sound area where natural, found, made, acoustic or electronic sources can be placed. Introduce a new sound source within an adult-led activity and afterwards, place the instrument in the sound area for the children to explore. Make sure the instruments are placed in accessible positions and make the area look visually exciting with pictures of instruments, labels for the activity of that week and other pictures, patterns and materials to stimulate exploration and composition.

Label a blank tape for each child with their name and a personal symbol and let them record some of their ideas. You can also use these tapes as 'note books' for each child, recording some of the music each child makes over a period of time.

Use the outside play area for music, from time to time, by using chalk to mark out musical games and activities.

## The role of the adult

You will play a crucial role in the children's musical activities, offering support and encouragement and valuing the children's responses, music-making and playing (especially when a child's choice of sounds might not match your own pre-conceived ideas!).

At this age, children are trying out many new sounds and may choose an instrument for its tactile or visual appearance as much as for its sound quality. It is important to maintain a balance between observing, participating, leading, explaining and acting as facilitator and enabler. Within the creative process it is sometimes difficult to know when to intervene; the temptation is always to 'improve' a child's composition by making suggestions.

The aim is to develop the children's ability to select and reject sounds and to make patterns without destroying their own contribution. At this stage, the process is far more important than any finished product.

## Choosing and using recorded music

Recorded music and songs should be chosen from a wide variety of styles and cultures including classical, pop, avant garde, jazz, folk, early music and music from around the world. Initially, select examples with which you are familiar in order to gain self confidence, but gradually expand the repertoire and range so that you are not simply passing on your own preferences to children.

Listen carefully to recordings beforehand and choose short sections in order to keep the children's attention. Play the piece or section a few times and return to it over the next weeks.

### Planning for progression in learning

Nurseries are required by OFSTED to show evidence of adequate planning and preparation within each learning area. Music as part of Creative Development must be included in this. The activities in this book do not form a scheme of work, nor do they imply a progression but can be taken as examples to fit into individual nursery's plans.

It is vitally important to plan and prepare for music in the same way as in other areas. Plan to provide a wide, varied and balanced programme which involves children in exploring all sound sources, in making their own music and in listening and responding to a wide variety of sounds and recorded music in different styles from around the world.

### Observation and assessment

Use your observations and recordings of children's responses, compositions, explorations and play with sound sources, to help you plan for progression in learning for each individual child. Observations can take place at a distance within the nursery or through your own participation in an activity with a child. You need to observe children exploring freely on their own, responding to tasks set or working with other children.

Make your observations on a regular basis for two or three minutes at a time and note down your comments. By selecting a few children each week, you will be able to build up a profile of each child and to understand more about the way they learn and engage in music, in creative activities and in other learning areas. Profiles should include children's written, drawn and movement responses to music together with tapes of their sound explorations and emergent compositions. Videotaping, if available, can provide an important means of observing children working in the creative area.

Observations can help you to assess a child's manipulative skills in holding and controlling an instrument, and their cognitive understanding of what they have listened to and made in music (for example a drum beat or fast, slow or quiet music). They will also help you to capture something of their expressive and imaginative responses.

### Equal opportunities

Children with special educational needs should be, as in other learning areas, integrated into all of the activities. Children can compose, listen and respond in non-verbal ways and because of this, the creative learning area is often one in which they excel, surpassing other children in their imaginative responses and sound creations. For those children with specific physical learning needs, electronic sound sources such as microphones, amplification units or sound pads can allow them to respond and create without difficulty.

### Links with home

Babies respond to music while they are still in the womb, so by the time children arrive in the nursery they will have listened and responded to a wide variety of music. A song or a piece of music associated with home can therefore be an invaluable bridge to starting work with children in the nursery.

Invite parents and carers to share songs and tapes which are important

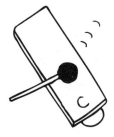

to their child, and to sing and share their own music from a variety of cultures. The Desirable Outcomes For Learning suggest that links with home should be a two-way process. Let children take home a tape of a new song or piece of music which they have used in the nursery, so that it can be listened to and shared in the car or at home.

Consider asking parents and carers to join you in music sessions within the nursery. Even if they do not participate in sessions they will be surprised and interested to watch their young children performing, composing and responding to music.

## Health and safety

Check the Health and Safety guidelines from your own school and local authority and make sure you are working within them.

Make sure that the junk materials used to make sound sources are clean and free from sharp edges and that no pieces are likely to fly off when the children shake them or strike them. Acoustic and electronic instruments should be introduced within an adult-led group situation and explanations given about their care and use.

Ensure that instruments are not balanced on top of each other and that beaters are kept lying flat, except when in use. Choose beaters which do not have removable heads and teach children not to place them in their mouths.

Some activities use electronic keyboards, tape recorders or microphones, for these use rechargeable batteries where possible or place the equipment on a table against the wall with the electric flex securely hidden and blocked. Activities are marked in the text with the note CARE! where particular caution is needed. If you are using a free-standing microphone, place it on a stand at the front with children well back and allow children to use the microphone one at a time.

## How to use this book

The book commences with a topic web which shows the activities for each learning area. A learning objective is given for each activity but there are also other cross-curricula objectives which may be identified and each activity contains an essential music learning objective.

For each activity, suggestions are made for an approximate group size (although the exact number will depend on your particular children and the number of adult helpers) and for the resources required. In most cases you will be able to substitute other instruments or sound sources for those listed. Advice is given on how to set up the activity and what to do with the children. Some of the activities may require more than one session. 'Questions to ask' are given to prompt discussion, and you will need to think of others bearing in mind that open-ended questions are generally more productive. Sensitivity is required when asking children about their feelings or imaginative responses.

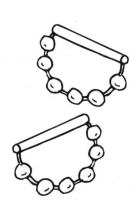

Suggestions for giving extra support and extension ideas for progression in learning are given for younger and older children. 'Follow-up activities' suggests other activities within the same learning area and also gives links to other areas of learning. At the end of the book there is a section of photocopiable materials.

# MUSIC

## CHAPTER ONE

*Involve children in letter recognition by playing with vocal sounds, support word identification with rhythmic activities and encourage children to make up their own stories to aid speaking and listening. Support early reading and writing skills as children develop their own symbol systems for sound.*

# ANIMAL PHONETICS

*Learning objective*
To learn the sound associated with the initial letter of some familiar animal names.

*Group size*
Six to eight children.

## What you need
Four pictures of different animals, four cards each with a corresponding initial letter for the animals. Adult helper.

## Setting up
Place the large card letters on the floor in front of you. Stick the pictures onto boards and place them on the floor, upright. Ask the children to sit in two groups all facing the front.

## What to do
Look at the animal pictures together and encourage the children to name the animals. Ask them if they know what letter the word starts with and demonstrate for them, encouraging them to join in. Look at the shape of the relevant letter in front of you and point to it while making the phonetic sound.

Next, explain that you are going to play a game in which the children have to guess which animal (out of the four pictures) you are thinking of, by listening carefully to the first letter sound. Give them an example, perhaps asking an adult helper to 'guess' which animal you are thinking of as you chant and repeat the first letter phonetically. Tell the children to decide which animal you have chosen. When a child successfully chooses the animal, encourage everyone to repeat and chant the word three or four times.

Now, encourage one group to repeat the first letter continuously whilst the other group repeats the whole word. The groups can do this after each other and then at the same time. Proceed in the same way with the letters and words for the other animals.

## Questions to ask
What animal is this? Can you join in with me saying the first letter? Which animal word begins with (letter)? Which animal am I thinking of? (As you reiterate the first letter). Can you say the animal's name with me?

## For younger children
Encourage younger children to join in and name the animal in each picture.

## For older children
Increase the number of animal pictures. Choose animals with the same first letters and draw attention to the similarity, for example cat, crocodile.

**Follow-up activities**
● Make a pattern using colours for the different first letters and count the number of times it is drawn in a row.
● Draw a large first letter and draw the animal inside the space.
● Tape record the phonetic sound of the first letters, place the tape in the sound area and ask children to match the sound to the pictures.

# FRUIT SALAD

**Learning objective**
*To recognize and use the names of fruits in rhythmic patterning.*

**Group size**
*Two to six children.*

## What you need
Some fruits (use only those with words of one or two syllables to begin with), for example plum, pear, grape, ap / ple, man / go, or / ange. Add three syllables when the children have some experience, such as ba / na / na, pine / ap / ple, straw / be / rry. Two tambourines (or made instruments which can be beaten rather than shaken), a cloth.

## Setting up
Lay out the fruits on a cloth on the floor and gather the children around you. Put the tambourines (or made instruments) beside you.

## What to do
Choose one fruit (with one syllable) and ask the children to name it. Encourage them to clap once while saying the name. Demonstrate and encourage them to join in. Pass a tambourine around the group and ask the children to play once while you say the name of the fruit. Demonstrate how to play the instrument while saying the word, before passing the instrument on. Ask them to play the tambourine while the rest of the group claps and says the word, repeating it a few times. Try this with different children playing the instruments.

Repeat this activity with other one syllable fruits and over a period of time introduce two and three syllable words. Clap the rhythm of the three syllable words as you would say them (in unequal patterns as they are used in speech, rather than making each syllable the same length).

## Questions to ask
Can you tell me the name of this fruit? Can we say the (fruit) together? Can you carry on saying (fruit) while I clap its name? Can you watch me and join in with the clapping? (Exaggerate your movements to make it easier.) Can you say (fruit) at the same time as clapping? Can you play the tambourine as we clap and say the word?

## For younger children
Encourage younger children to recognize and name the fruits, saying the word with you while you clap.

## For older children
Encourage older children to clap or play two and three syllable words. Ask them to try two words of differing syllables one after the other.

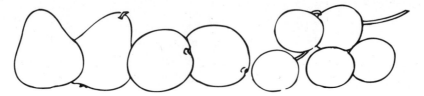

**Follow up activities**
● Make a musical score by drawing different fruit on a long strip of paper (use simple outline shapes coloured in). Clap and play the score, encouraging children to name the fruits first of all.
● Draw and paint pictures of oranges, apples, bananas and grapes, selecting appropriate colours.
● Make a cube with fruit on each face (see maths activity photocopiable page 60) and play the game by naming and then clapping the fruit pictured on top.

# STORM MUSIC

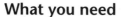

**Learning objective**
*To have a discussion about a storm, developing appropriate language.*

**Group size**
*Six to eight children.*

## What you need
A selection of instruments including child-made shakers and sound makers. Pictures of rain, dark cloudy skies and clear blue skies. Tape recording of rain falling, thunder and howling wind.

## Setting up
Play your tape and get used to the tape recorder functions and the sounds that you have recorded. Set up the tape recorder near to you (CARE!). Set up the colour pictures around you and put a selection of instruments on the floor. Gather the children around them in a circle.

## What to do
Play a tape recording of part of a storm (one minute approximately) and look at the weather pictures, drawing attention to what is happening in each one. Question and encourage the children to respond, developing appropriate language and vocabulary.

Now play a drum loudly and talk about thunder. Play a tambourine quietly by flicking your fingers onto the surface. Ask the children to tell you which is the thunder and which is the rain. Pass the instruments to one child at a time and ask them to make rain or thunder sounds.

## Questions to ask
How does the rain sound when it starts? Is it loud or quiet? Can you make the rain sound on this shaker/tambourine? Can you make a loud sound on the drum for the thunder? What is the wind like in a storm? What do you feel like when there is a storm? What happens after a storm? When you go out to play after a storm, what do you see on the ground?

## For younger children

Concentrate on words to do with the rain. Ask the children to tell you what is happening in the rain pictures and encourage them to make some sounds for themselves.

## For older children
Encourage older children to talk about the whole passage of the storm coming nearer and then going away. They can be encouraged to make sounds for the whole storm process.

**Follow-up activities**
● Paint pictures of a storm.
● Move around outdoors pretending to be the wind.
● Look at puddles after the rain and talk about them.
● Make copies of photocopiable page 59, laminate them and put them in the sound area for the children to use to make some music in response to the picture clues.

# BUS RIDE

*Learning objective*
*To make up a sound*
*story about a bus ride.*

*Group size*
*Four to six children.*

## What you need
Pictures of a bus and a bus driver, coins and a bag, a hat for the bus driver and the ticket inspector, eight chairs, a bell, pieces of paper (for tickets).

## Setting up.
Arrange the chairs in pairs leaving a space between each (the aisle). Place one chair on its own at the front for the driver. Put the pictures at the front and have the other items nearby ready to give out.

## What to do
Explain to the children that you are going to play at being on a bus. Look at the pictures you have available, encouraging the children to notice and name things. Seat the children on 'the bus', choose one child to role play the driver and one to play the ticket inspector and give them the hats, bag and money. Explain that they will all have a turn at driving or being the ticket inspector. Talk about what the driver and inspector do on a bus. Encourage the children to get on, get off, pay for a ticket, hand over a ticket and coins, drive the bus and inspect the tickets. Talk about who gets on the bus.

Once the children can do this, encourage them to make sounds to match what is happening such as vocal sounds while the bus is revving up and driving off (demonstrate with your voice and encourage them to join in), shaking the bells when a passenger wants to get off, rattling the coins and banging a drum for the doors slamming.

Once the children have been introduced to this activity, they can make up their own stories and sequences about what is happening on the bus using the sounds to support their role play.

## Questions to ask
What colour is the bus? Where does the driver sit? How do you get a ticket? Who gets on the bus? Who looks at the tickets? What should you do as soon as you have your ticket? How do you stop the bus? Can you make the sound of the bus revving up and starting? Can you make the bell sound? What sound can you make for the doors slamming?

## For younger children
Younger children can talk about the bus stopping and starting and practise ringing the bell to make the bus stop and start. They can be encouraged to join in with the role play.

## For older children
Older children can contribute their own sounds and ideas and can sequence the sounds. They can be encouraged to contribute ideas about the different passengers who get on and off the bus.

**Follow up activities**
● Make a bus stop sign and labels for the bus destination. Encourage children to contribute their own ideas for stops such as school, bus station, shops or the park.
● Draw numbers on tickets. Exchange them for the same number of coins from another child.
● Make a collage of a bus, with a bus queue of different people.

# SINGING LETTERS

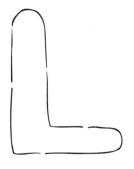

### Learning objective
*To make the movements required in making and shaping letters.*

### Group size
*One to three children.*

## What you need
Large letters drawn on pieces of card; almost as big as child height (select letters with which the children are familiar), sand tray area.

## Setting up
Before starting, read through the activity carefully and practise your own vocal sounds for each letter. Try them out with some colleagues and see what they think (there is no right or wrong interpretation!). Place the large letters upright beside the sand area. Smooth over the dampened sand to make it as flat as possible.

## What to do
Gather the children to the sand area. Select one letter at a time, starting with a familiar letter for each child, and encourage the children to name the letter. Explain that today they will hear the letter and sing its shape. Articulate the beginning of each letter with its phonetic sound (as you would do normally) and then hum or sing the shape of the letter with rise and fall of pitch according to how the letter shape is made. For example a letter L (upper case) will start high and slide down low, then stay on the same note, a letter 'm' (lower case) will slide up, down, up and down.

As you hum or sing, make the shape of the letter in the air. Encourage the children to draw the shape in the air and in the sand and to hum or sing at the same time. Encourage them to listen to you and then to join in themselves, offering their own contributions.

## Questions to ask
Can you tell me what letter this is? Let's all say it! (Use phonetic pronunciation.) Can you trace its shape in the air/in the sand? Listen to this letter singing! Can you hear it? Watch and listen whilst I trace the shape. (Hum or sing.) Can you join in? Can you trace the letter in the air/ on the card /in the sand and make it sing? Can you hear the sound changing as it goes up high and falls down low? Can you make it do that? Can you try to make your own name in the sand and sing the letters?

## For younger children
Concentrate on one or two letters for each child. Encourage them to draw the shape with their finger on the letter card or in the sand. They can be encouraged to make vocal sounds by concentrating on the beginning phonetic sound. Do not worry if their further vocalizing bears no resemblance to your ideas.

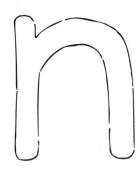

## For older children
Encourage them to draw in the air and sand, join in with you and contribute their own sounds. Encourage them to sing with you as a group whilst making the shapes. Ask them to listen to each other's sounds and copy them.

### Follow-up activities
● Make the movement required for each letter with the whole body; for letter 'm' crouching down low, going high, then low, high and back to a crouch.
● With the whole group, make letter shapes with whole bodies by lying on the floor.
● Paint letters on large sheets of paper and decorate them with collage materials, glitter or screwed-up tissue paper.

# SINGING PUPPETS

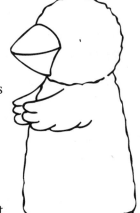

*Learning objective*
To recognize and learn
own and other people's
names.

*Group size*
Six to eight children.

## What you need
Puppets with beaks or mouths that can be articulated or with arms that can be easily moved, the tune 'Skip to my Lou'.

## Setting up
Practise singing or chanting to the tune of 'Skip to my Lou':
   *Hello everyone, how are you?* (three times)
   *How are you today?*
Do not worry about the pitch of the tune, if you do not feel confident chant or make up a tune of your own. Put the puppets in a bag or box beside you.

## What to do
Explain that you are meeting some new friends today and they are in a bag beside you. (Once the children know the puppets, encourage them to guess which one is coming out first.) Introduce the children to today's puppet, naming him and asking them to notice features about him (colour, number of eyes, whiskers). Tell them that the puppet is going to sing to them:
   *He-llo Ma-ry, how are you* (times three)
   *How are you to-day?*
   As you sing, move the arms or beaks of the puppet for each syllable, keeping it closed for longer on the last word of each line.
   Ask the children to watch the puppet's beak or arms as you sing. Encourage them to join in with the beak movement using their hands as they watch and then to join in with the singing.
   As the puppet meets each child, let the child touch him and make the puppet have a small conversation. Make it fun so that the children are encouraged to respond. For example the puppet meets Tom and says, 'I like your trainers, I could do with some!' and let the puppet laugh! Eventually encourage the children to reply on the last line:
   *I'm all right today!*

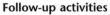

## Questions to ask
Who do you think is in the bag? How many paws, eyes, has he got? Can you see his beak moving as he sings? Can you join in with him using your hands? He is going to sing to each of you in turn. Can you sing with him as he sings to (name)? Can you reply to him?

## For younger children
Younger children can role play the beak movement as the puppet sings. They can respond to the puppet by stroking him or shaking his paw if they do not reply or sing.

## For older children
Encourage older children to reply with their own answers about how they feel and to sing and do the beak movement at the same time.

### Follow-up activities
● Put the puppet(s) in the sound activity area for children to play with. Ask them to make the puppet sing 'hello' to another child.
● Make up a story using the puppets as central characters.
● Move around like the puppet animal: crocodile, panda, monkey, bear.

# VOCAL GYMNASTICS

*Learning objective*
*To develop confidence in using voices.*

*Group size*
*Two to four children.*

## What you need
A microphone and amplifier – some tape recorders have built-in amplifiers (not essential but useful), white board or large sheet of white paper and coloured felt-tipped pens.

## Setting up
Practise making vocal sounds yourself until you feel confident. Arrange the white board or large paper sheets at the front, place the microphone and amplifier at the front near to the board.(CARE!)

## What to do
Group the children in a semi circle around the board. Explain that you are going to play a game with your voices and demonstrate making different sounds of pitch, volume and speed. Demonstrate with nonsense words or cartoon exclamations such as Zoom! (said or sung quickly), Ker plunk! (two different pitches) and WHEeee (loud becoming quieter).

Encourage the children to join in and use the microphone if they wish. Using the board, ask them to watch the line as you draw. Ask them to look at the line and tell you what it is doing (for example going up or down). Make some 'wiggly' lines and match them with wiggly vocal sounds. Draw a line going up and down and slide your voice up and down as you do so. Draw some small dots at random and make some small dots of sound to match.

## Question to ask
Can you join in with me? Can you make a sound yourself? Can you follow this shape with me (drawing a finger or stick along a shaped line). Can you sing the shape with me. What does the line do? (Goes up, down.) Draw some lines such as a large black circle with jagged edges, a line going up, a curved line, lots of little dots. Ask: what do you think this sounds like?

## For younger children
Encourage children to join in with the sounds, using the microphone and copying your sounds when they can. Do not worry too much about the corresponding symbols.

## For older children
Older children can be encouraged to make their own suggestions and to copy each other's suggestions, joining in as a group.

**Follow-up activities**
● Encourage children to freely explore this idea on their own in the sound area, using voice or instruments.
● Draw a line or shape and record a sound to go with it.
● Speak into the microphone to make announcements such as: It's milk time now! Now we have to clear up! Today is William's birthday!

# SOUND RHYMES

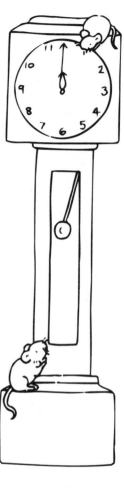

*Learning objective*
*To observe a repeated pattern of words.*

*Group size*
*Two to six children.*

### What you need
A selection of unpitched percussion instruments (one each for every child) and a selection of rhymes which have repeated sections of words such as 'Hickory, Dickory Dock'. Write the rhymes down or have them in your mind to use.

### Setting up
Put the instruments in front of you.

### What to do

Group the children around you and tell them that you are going to sing some rhymes. Draw attention to the repetition in each rhyme by clapping or playing an instrument when a pattern of words is repeated. Next, ask the children if they can tell you for which words the instruments are played. Explain that the words are the same each time, repeat the rhyme and ask them to clap throughout the repeated phrases, exaggerating your hand movement prior to each phrase so that they can pick up the cue and join in.

Next, give each child an instrument, explain that it is sleeping and quiet unless the words are spoken/sung, when it must be played. Try out some of the rhymes and encourage the children to shake or bang their instruments when the words or phrases are repeated.

### For younger children
Provide instruments which can be easily shaken for younger children (bells, shakers). Concentrate on one poem or rhyme which has short lines and two or three words as repetition (such as 'Humpty Dumpty').

### For older children
Older children can make up sounds with a different instrument for the rest of the rhyme and listen to the repetition of more complex phrases. Split the children into two groups encouraging some to play an instrument for all of the words except the repetition, and others to play a different instrument during the repetition.

**Follow-up activities**
● Add movements to the repeated sections of words.
● Draw pictures of a favourite rhyme.
● Make a repeating pattern using crayons, paints, papers.

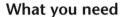

*Children can encounter a range of mathematical concepts through musical play activities. These examples are designed to encourage the use of mathematical language and will involve children in patterning, sorting, counting, sequencing and matching.*

# MUSICAL SANDWICHES

**Learning objective**
*To develop an understanding of pattern and sequence.*

**Group size**
*Six to eight children.*

### What you need
Unpitched percussion instruments or sound makers made by the children. Pictures of sandwiches, a tray, knife, bread slices, margarine/butter, and a sandwich filling.

### Setting up
Put the food and knife on a tray beside you. (CARE!) Mount the pictures of sandwiches on the wall at child height. Gather the children around in a circle and place the instruments in the middle.

### What to do
Talk about sandwiches and use the food and knife to make one as you talk. Ask the children to role play the actions along with you. Encourage them to understand that bread is the same on top and underneath the sandwich whereas the filling is something which goes inside and is different (or *not* the same). Explain that we can make a musical sandwich with two sounds the same for the bread and a different sound for the filling inside. Lay out three instruments in front of you (tambourine, bells, tambourine) in a row and play them one after the other. Ask the children which ones are the same. Explain that these are the same, like the bread.

Make another musical sandwich with a different 'filling' and then ask individual children to choose and play 'fillings', 'bread' and 'whole sandwiches' according to their understanding, moving from their place into the middle of the circle to do so.

### Questions to ask
What do we need to make a sandwich? How many pieces of bread? What filling can we have? What sounds can we have for our musical sandwiches? What instrument can you choose for the filling?

### For younger children
Younger children can suggest a filling and play their filling sound, exploring different sounds for different fillings. They might not make the connection between the sound and the filling but can be encouraged to choose different instruments and to explore the sounds.

### For older children
Older children can make whole musical sandwiches putting instruments and sounds together in a sequence.

**Follow-up activities**
● Older children can draw their own symbols for their sandwich.
● Place the children's drawings in the sound area for others to play.
● Make sandwiches out of junk material (polystyrene for the bread and tissue for the filling).

# HOOP-LA

*Learning objective*
To sort wood and metal instruments and sound makers.

*Group size*
Two to six children.

## What you need
Wooden instruments: claves, wooden guiro, wooden gato drum, wooden agogo, twigs, sticks, logs. Metal instruments: triangle, metal guiro, metal agogo, bells, saucepan lids, keys, coins. Two hoops or two large sheets of card, two large labels 'wood' and 'metal', a tape recorder and blank tape.

## Setting up
Ensure that each instrument/sound source is only made from one material; a tambourine made of skin, wood and metal is too difficult to sort for this initial activity. Place a hoop flat on the floor on either side of the instruments and gather the children around.

## What to do
Select one wooden instrument, make a few sounds on it and then ensure that each child makes a sound on it, feels it, looks at it and listens to it, encouraging them with questions and observations. Name the instrument and describe what wood is and where it comes from.
Repeat the process with each of the wooden instruments and then continue with the metal instruments.

Explain that you are going to sort the instruments by placing the wooden instruments inside one hoop and the metal instruments inside the other hoop. Initially start with four or five instruments to sort. When these have been sorted, gather two or three children by each hoop and let them explore the instruments, developing language in response to questions.

Let each group make some sounds with the instruments and tape-record a few seconds from each group. Play the recording back to the children and ask them to describe the category they are listening to.

## Questions to ask
What is the (name the instrument) made of? What does it feel like? Can you make a sound on it? Do you like the feel and the sound of this? Where does wood come from? Can you feel the metal instrument? What does it feel like? Are the bells cold or hot when you touch them?

## For younger children
Encourage younger children to explore the instruments, becoming accustomed to the sounds, feel and appearance of each. Let them sort the wooden instruments first, using one hoop.

## For older children
Older children can be encouraged to identify the material of the instrument and to name it. Ask them to sort the instruments into two sets, increasing the number of instruments in the activity over a period of time.

**Follow-up activities**
● Explore three or four instruments of one material (labelled) in the sound area.
● Draw the instruments and tape record their sounds.
● Move around to the sound of wood and metal instruments.
● Add wooden or metal sounds to a story about the home.

# WATER BOTTLES

*Learning objective*
To encourage understanding of quantity and the terms 'more than' and 'less than'.

*Group size*
Two to six children.

## What you need
Identical plastic, transparent bottles (two for each child), 'beaters' made of soft and hard materials (sticks, drum sticks, xylophone beaters) – if you do not have these, improvise by attaching material round the end of a paint brush to make a soft beater and use the stick end of the paint brush for a hard beater.

## Setting up
Prepare the children for water play, wearing overalls or aprons and with sleeves rolled up. Position bottles in the water area.

## What to do
Ask children to explore filling and emptying the bottles, observing, touching and listening to the water sounds. Work with the children, filling one water bottle and asking the children to fill one. Then hold up an empty bottle and ask them to show you their empty bottle. When the children can do this, pour a small amount into one bottle, ask them to match this and then show one with 'more' water in. Encourage them to fill two bottles, filling the second with 'more' water.

Encourage the children to observe, talk about what they see, feel the water and listen to the sounds. Place bottles containing different amounts of water on a flat surface and hit them with a 'beater' listening carefully to the different sounds they make.

## Questions to ask
Can you fill the bottle with water? Can you empty the bottle? Is the bottle full, empty? Can you pour more water into this bottle? What sound does it make? Can you tell me about it? Do you like it? Do the bottles sound the same? Is there more water in this bottle? Which sound do you like?

## For younger children
Younger children can explore the water and bottles, filling and emptying, listening to the sounds and developing the language of full and empty. They can talk about the sounds and listen to the differences.

## For older children
Older children can be encouraged to observe smaller differences and to fill their own bottles with different amounts. They can compare their own bottles with those of another child and listen to the different sounds.

**Follow-up activities**
● Colour in bottle outlines on a card.
● Fill plastic bottles with coloured beads (cut tops off bottles and cover sharp edges with masking tape).
● Suspend the bottles from a rail and play them with beaters, observing the different sounds.
● Tape record the filling and emptying sounds.

# MYSTERY MATCHING

*Learning objective*
*To match and play sounds with and without visual cues.*

*Group size*
*Four to six children.*

## What you need
Eight instruments (two of each), pictures of instruments, a table and brightly coloured cloth.

## Setting up
Drape the table with a brightly coloured cloth and sew or stick pictures of instruments onto it to act as a screen. Gather the children in a circle sitting on the floor. Place four of the instruments in the middle of the circle and the matching four beside you.

## What to do
Choose an instrument from those beside you and play some sounds with it. Ask the children to come into the middle one at a time and find the matching instrument. Encourage the child to play the instrument and involve all of the children in talking about it. Draw attention to the pictures on the screen and ask the children if they can see another one the same on it. If a child does not select an identical instrument, it is important to praise the sounds which have been made. Encourage the child to talk about the sounds made.

Once children are familiar with the sounds, hide four instruments behind the screen leaving the matching four in front where the children can see them. Play an instrument behind the screen and ask a child to choose and play one which is the same.

To begin with play the instruments in turn but gradually, as the children develop understanding, mix up the order with some repetitions of sounds to make the task more difficult.

## Questions to ask
What is this instrument called? Do you like the sound? Can you shake your hands or pat your legs when I play it? What does it feel like? Is it smooth, shiny, hard, soft, brown, black and so on? Can you find another one the same? Which one do you like best?

### For younger children
Younger children might not choose the identical instrument and might find it difficult when the visual cue has been removed (instrument hidden). They can be encouraged to explore, develop language and touch the instruments, telling you what they like and how they make them feel.

### For older children
Older children can gradually try to match more instruments, perhaps exploring one new instrument each time. They can take turns at being the leader behind the mystery screen.

**Follow-up activities**
● Make cards with pictures of instruments for children to match individually.
● Using only the instruments which have already been explored, give each child one of a matching pair. Ask the children to move around and try to find the child who has the same instrument.
● Listen to the sounds of instruments on tape and match with a picture card or instrument.

# BAKE A CAKE

*Learning objective*
*To add the ingredients used in making a cake, developing mathematical language.*

*Group size*
*One to six children.*

## What you need
Pictures of cakes and ingredients, packets labelled with some of the ingredients, a bowl and mixing spoon.

## Setting up
Gather the children into the home corner with the pictures, ingredients, bowl and spoon. Practise making sounds associated with making a cake yourself.

## What to do
Talk about making a cake and the ingredients which you might use. Role play making and baking a cake using the actions for pouring, adding, mixing, switching on the oven, taking out, cutting and sharing the cake. Once the children have role played the actions, explain that you want them to make some sounds to go with the actions.

Encourage children to make sounds with their voices and bodies (no musical instruments). Encourage each child to make up a different sound and action. Explain and show the children how to hum when the oven is heating and demonstrate clicking sounds for the switch sounds. Make a lot of sounds yourself and encourage them to have fun exploring their own sounds.

Name the ingredients as the first, second and so on. Ask the children which is the first thing we need for the cake mix. When the 'ingredients' have been added, make another similar 'cake', developing the children's understanding of the language involved. Listen to the sounds suggested by the children, questioning and developing the same mathematical language.

## Questions to ask
What kind of cake do you like? What do we need to make a cake? Which is the first thing needed for the cake mix? Which is the second? Can you count all the things we have put in the cake? How does the oven sound when it is cooking the cake? Can you put your lips together and hum? What sounds can you make as we mix/beat the eggs/pour the milk?

## For younger children
Younger children can be encouraged to learn the names of the ingredients and to make the actions for preparing and baking a cake. They will be able to make some of the sounds associated with the actions. Develop their counting skills from one to five.

## For older children
Ask older children to count and name the ingredients, make the actions and sounds and begin to use the language of order. Encourage them to sequence and memorize the sounds which occur in the process of making a cake.

**Follow-up activities**
● Tape record the sounds for the cake making and baking. Play them back to the children and ask them to count and order them.
● Make a cake out of modelling clay, cut out pieces, count and order.
● Encourage the children to make their own musical food in the sound area.
● Make up a story about a person baking a birthday cake and ask the children to add the sounds.

# MUSIC CUBE

**Learning objective**
*To match sounds to different numbers and symbols on the faces of a cube.*

**Group size**
*One to six children.*

## What you need
A large cube (dice), pictures/symbols of six different instruments. Six instruments which match the pictures on the cube. Photocopiable page 60.

## Setting up
Make a large cube (dice) out of stiff cardboard or a box, using photocopiable page 60 as a guide. Stick pictures of instruments on each face of the cube. Alternatively make the cube from fabric and stuff it, marking the instruments on with felt-tipped pens or fabric paint. Seat the children in a circle on the floor with enough space in the middle to place the six instruments and to throw the cube.

## What to do
Play sounds on one instrument and then hand it to each child to make their own sounds. Repeat with the other five instruments, encouraging the children to name, play, feel, touch and develop language about the instruments.

Next bring out the cube and encourage the children to talk about it; name and play each instrument that they recognize. Explain that the top picture of the musical cube will show them which instrument to play. Point to the top as you explain this. Throw the dice and ask one child to find the instrument which is the same as the picture on the top. If they do not know which one it is, draw their attention to specific features (colour, shape). If they do not wish to choose an instrument, encourage them to talk about the symbol.

## Questions to ask
What instruments can you see on the cube? Can you make some sounds on this instrument? Do you like this instrument?(Name it.) Can you draw round the tambourine with your finger? Is it round, square? Can you draw round the triangle? Can you see the triangle on the cube?

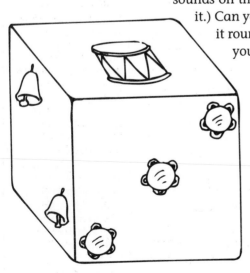

## For younger children
Younger children might not be able to name the instruments. They should be encouraged to make the sounds but might not be able to match them to the symbols. Encourage them to draw with their finger around the shapes.

## For older children
Ask older children to match and play the appropriate instrument, making more sounds on the instrument and playing it in different ways.

---

**Follow-up activities**
● Make another cube with numbers instead of instruments (one to six). Ask the children to recognize and name the numbers. Play a wood block or drum, counting the number of beats to match the number on the cube.
● Play the game with both dice, finding the matching instrument and hitting or shaking it the number of times indicated on the second cube.
● Encourage children to make their own cube, adding number or picture symbols. (Using photocopiable page 60.)

# ISLANDS

## What you need
Large sheets of coloured card, paper or fabric, scissors, sand tray, a tambourine or a tape of recorded music (any music – vary it on subsequent occasions), a tape recorder.

## Setting up
Cut circle and square shapes from the same colour and material, so that the only difference is the shape. They should each be large enough to provide sitting space for a child).Provide enough for one circle and one square for each child. Spread the shapes out in a large area (hall, large space, playground) keeping the circles in one area and the squares in another to begin with.

## What to do
Set the scene for the children before moving to the large space. Show them a circle and a square and encourage them to trace the outline of both shapes in the air or in the sand.

Explain that when you go to the area, you will play some music and they must move around the space without treading on an island (circle island and square island). Once there, demonstrate to the children how to move around without touching the islands.

Next ask the children to walk around very carefully and slowly without touching an island. When they can do this, encourage them to move around to music, stopping when the music stops, finding an island and sitting down on it. Use either the recorded music or play the tambourine. Repeat this several times. On each occasion, when the children are sitting down, ask individual children which island they are sitting on (square or circle).

The next stage in the game is to hold up a shape when the music stops to indicate which shape of island the children must occupy. If children sit on a wrong shaped island, take your shape over to them and ask them to notice differences and to trace the shapes again.

## Questions to ask
Can you draw round the circle on the floor/in the air with your hand? Can you walk round the outside of the square without touching it? Can you stop when the music stops and sit on the floor? Who else is sitting on a circle island?

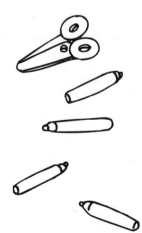

## For younger children
Younger children can be encouraged to move around avoiding the islands. They might not be able to differentiate between the shapes but should be encouraged to find an island to sit on.

## For older children
Older children will find it most difficult when the shapes are mixed up on the floor, so make the random distribution increasingly complex.

### Follow-up activities
● Play the game to encourage movements of imaginary turtles swimming in the sea and sleeping on islands.
● Cut out squares and circles, stick them onto card to make patterns.
● Look at pictures and find circles and squares in them.
● Cut out circles and squares and suspend them on string or ribbon from the ceiling.

# COUNTING SOUNDS

*Learning objective*
*To count the number of sounds in each set, recorded on a tape.*

*Group size*
*One to six children.*

## What you need
A tape of common sounds (see Setting up), a tape recorder, a drum and drum stick or beater and beads for counting, pictures of the recorded sound sources.

## Setting up
Prepare a tape in advance grouping sounds into sets (house sounds, animal sounds, body sounds and so on). Record each set twice and leave spaces of a few seconds between each set. Keep the sounds reasonably short and finite such as a door slamming, car horn or a cat miaowing rather than continuous sounds such as running water.

## Setting up
Sit at some tables with the children in a group. Ensure that each child has beads or blocks with which to count. Place the tape recorder and drum nearby. Put the pictures up on the wall.

## What to do
Ask the children to count the sounds as you beat a drum slowly, counting aloud yourself. Make one beat to begin with, then two, three and so on.

Play the first sound of the first recorded set, show the corresponding picture to the children and encourage them to name it. Then as each sound is played, ask the children to move a block into a pile in front of them. When each example has been played, ask the children to count their blocks.

## Questions to ask
Do you know what makes this sound? Can you show me the picture of it? How many beads or blocks have you moved? Can you count one, two? Can you clap your hands once as you say one? (Demonstrate.) Can you clap twice and say one, two? (Demonstrate.) How many times did the cat miaow?

## For younger children
Younger children might not at first be able to associate the audio sounds with counting. Encourage them to try to role play the sound where possible and help them to move their counters each time the sound is repeated.

## For older children
Let older children synchronize their claps or beats as they say the numbers and clap or beat the number of times they heard the sound after it has been played.

### Follow-up activities
● Place a tape recorder with a counting sound tape in the sound area for children to explore individually. (CARE!)
● Play the tape near the sand area and let the children make the numbers in the sand after they have listened to each example.
● Let children choose their own instrument or sound maker and record the sounds that they make for each number.

*CHAPTER THREE*

*Musical role play activities can encourage children to become involved in sharing, taking turns and developing sensitivity towards people of other cultures and those who have different physical abilities from themselves. These examples will also help children to think about living creatures with care and concern and to express their feelings.*

# TEA PARTY

***Learning objective***
*To co-operate in a group.*

***Group size***
*Three to four children.*

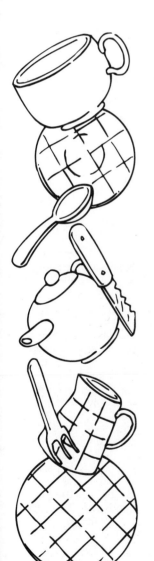

## What you need
A kettle, cups and saucers, teaspoons, sugar bowl, milk jug, teapot, water. Tape recorder and blank tape.

## Setting up
Gather the children together in the home area. Encourage them to sit on chairs around a table and place all of the items for the tea party on the table. Put the tape recorder near to you. (CARE!)

## What to do
Ask the children to think about making a cup of tea. Pour some water into the kettle and role play waiting for it to boil, putting tea bags and water into the pot, pouring out the tea and adding sugar and milk. Ask the children questions throughout about what to do next and act in response to their replies. Encourage the children to pass the cups to each other and to say 'thank you'. Role play drinking the tea, handing back the cups and washing them up afterwards.

At each stage encourage children to listen carefully to the sounds which are being made:
• water being poured into the kettle;
• the kettle boiling (make vocal sounds of bubbling);
• cups being put down on saucers;
• teaspoons stirring the sugar in cups.
Ask the children to repeat some of the sounds and make a recording.

## Questions to ask
What do we put in a pot of tea? What do we do first? Can you make the sound of water being poured into the pot/the bubbling sounds as the kettle boils? Would you like milk/sugar in your tea? Listen to the stirring sound. When (name) passes you the cup what do you say?

## For younger children
Younger children might not role play the whole sequence but can be encouraged to concentrate on one or two actions and sounds.

## For older children
Older children will be able to sequence the actions and sounds more easily and to remember more of them. Start with two or three sounds one after the other and gradually encourage them to remember more.

**Follow-up activities**
● Play the tape of sounds back to the children at a later date and talk about what is happening as each sound is played. Place the tape labelled with a tea pot symbol in the sound area for children to listen to.
● Draw and make collages of a teapot and a cup.
● Role play making other drinks from different cultures.

# CONDUCTOR

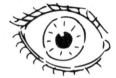

*Learning objective*
To develop sensitivity towards people of all physical attributes and abilities.

*Group size*
Three to five children.

## What you need
Sound makers or instruments, one for each child.

## Setting up
Collect the children into a semi-circle and place the instruments and sound makers in front of you.

## What to do
Explain that the children must watch your hands carefully. When you move your hands, they can shake or bang their instrument and when you put your hands down they must stop playing and be quiet. Give an instrument to each child (use instruments with which they are already familiar). Put your hands together in your lap and explain again that they must be very still and watch.

Next, explain that there are many people who are unable to move some parts of their bodies – some people cannot move their arms but they can conduct with their feet or heads, some people cannot move their legs but can move their arms while sitting down.

Explain to the children that you are now going to move different parts of your body and they must watch very carefully. When they see your arm or leg move, they can play and when it stops moving, they must stop playing. Begin by using large, easily observed movements (a foot waggling or a head moving) and as the children's observations become more acute, use smaller and finer movements (a finger or wrist moving or an eye blinking). Ensure that they understand by watching their response with the instruments.

Once the children can do this, let them take turns at being the conductor themselves, conducting with different parts of their bodies.

If you have children within the group who have specific physical abilities this activity can, if intorduced with sensitvity, offer them a huge sense of confidence.

## Questions to ask
Can you keep your hands very still? When you see my hands move can you pick up your instrument and shake/bang it? Can you stop when I stop? Can you shake your instrument when (child's name) shakes his/her arms? Which part of the body is (name) moving? Have I stopped moving my foot/head?

## For younger children
Allow younger children plenty of practise in playing their instruments in response to your large movement cues. Encourage them to watch carefully.

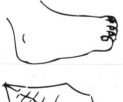

## For older children
Encourage them to stop and start exactly on cue using a variety of instruments. Develop their observation of smaller movements as cues.

**Follow-up activities**
● Watch a short piece of a video showing a conductor with an orchestra.
● Make up or find a story about a person who cannot move easily and has to travel by wheelchair, or an animal who has three instead of four legs. Read or tell the story to the children and talk about the feelings of the person or animal.
● Show pictures of hands or feet and ask the children to play their shaker with the part of the body shown.

# HIDDEN VOICE

**Learning objective**
*To understand, recognize and value the fact that everyone has a different voice.*

**Group size**
*Three to six children.*

## What you need
A screen, big enough for a child to be hidden behind (a table covered in a cloth).

## Setting up
Set up the screen in front of the group of children. Alternatively, it might be possible to use the home area.

## What to do
Begin by sharing some rhymes or songs or by using topical words or chants with which the children are familiar. Sing or say these together so that they will be able to respond easily when you play the game. If there are particularly shy children, try to encourage them with words that are relevant to themselves. Try to encourage children to speak or sing individually so that everyone can listen to their voices.

Explain to the children that they are going to play 'Hide and seek' with their voices and that they will need to sit still and listen carefully. Explain that one child will go behind the screen and 'hide'. You will then tap one of the children in the group and he/she must sing or say a rhyme. The child behind the screen must guess who it is that is singing.

Place one child behind the screen and then choose one child from within the group by tapping them gently. Chant or sing together:
*Who is singing, who is singing* (speaking), *who is it?*

The child behind the screen has to guess who it is singing. When he/she has guessed, lead them from behind the screen and show them who the singer was. The child who sang or spoke can then repeat their song or words. As each child speaks or sings, talk about their voices, drawing attention to any noticeable features in a positive way.

## Questions to ask
Who do you think is speaking/singing? How do you know it is his/her (name) voice? Is his/her voice quiet or loud? Is his/her voice high? (Demonstrate with a high voice.) Does he/she (name) speak/sing quietly or loudly? Do you think it is a boy or a girl?

## For younger children
Younger children might be less inclined to join in with this game but can still try to guess who it is. They might need an adult helper to prompt and ask questions behind the screen. They will find it more difficult to recognize voices if they have not been in the nursery setting for long.

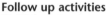

## For older children
Older children will be able to guess more easily and you will be able to encourage more detailed observations about the voices. Once they can do this activity in a small group, the group size can be increased to make it more difficult.

**Follow up activities**
● Make a tape recording of different voices (men, women and babies) using children's parents, carers and other family members. Encourage the children to listen to the tape and to talk about the differences in the voices.
● Cut out pictures of men, women, babies and children and ask the children to select which one they think matches the sound on tape. Include one or two examples of languages other than English.
● Invite male and female adults (parents, carers and helpers) to read a short story to the children so that they can listen to many different voices.

# HAMSTER MUSIC

*Learning objective*
*To treat a living animal*
*with care and*
*sensitivity.*

*Group size*
*Three to six children.*

## What you need
A hamster (or other small animal) in a cage. Unpitched percussion instruments (tambourine, bells, maracas, guiros) or child-made instruments. Pitched instruments such as xylophone and glockenspiel (with beaters) for more variety. Photocopiable page 61.

## What to do
Seat the children in a semi-circle, telling them that you are going to look at a hamster and that they must be very quiet. Explain why, if they are uncertain. Say that they are going to watch his movements.

Next bring the hamster in the cage to the front of the group. Encourage children to whisper or talk very quietly about him by doing so yourself. Talk about his movements or lack of them and ask questions. After a few minutes, remove the cage to a quiet place.

Next, explain that you are going to make up some music for the sleeping hamster. Using photocopiable page 61, encourage them to make suggestions and value their contributions, even if they do not match with your own ideas. Talk to them about the need for the music to be quiet rather than loud. Play some very loud sounds on the tambourine yourself and then some quiet sounds. Ask them which they think would be best to match the sleeping hamster picture. Pass an instrument to each child and encourage them to experiment. Do not intervene too much but observe, offering praise and comments.

The activity can progress to making 'moving hamster music' to reflect fast scurrying movements. Use the picture of the hamster running and playing and talk about what he is doing. Again demonstrate some scurrying, fast music yourself, encourage children to experiment and select sounds themselves, observe from a distance and then move back to praise and comment.If the hamster is asleep when you first observe him, compose the sleeping music first. If he is running around then compose the fast, scurrying music first.

## Questions to ask
Why should we be quiet when we look at the hamster? What sounds can we make for some sleeping music? Like this? (As you play loud, fast music.) Can you play some quiet sounds? What sounds can we make for the hamster as he scurries about/plays on his wheel? Is this running music?(As you play slow, very quiet sounds.)

## For younger children
Younger children will probably be able to make fast, loud sounds more easily to begin with. They will not be able to control making slow and quiet sounds at the same time.

## For older children
Older children might offer suggestions for both running and sleeping music. See if they can sequence this by playing one before the other.

---

**Follow-up activities**
● Paint pictures of the hamster (based on the real animal or the photocopied sheet).
● Try some hamster movements – scurrying around and then curling up in a ball to go to sleep while you play on an instrument (make fast or slow sounds).
● Write a group story about a hamster, adding emergent writing to the photocopied sheet or making a book together.

# MAGIC DRUM

*Learning objective*
*To take turns and pass an instrument to another child.*

*Group size*
*Six to eight children.*

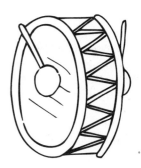

## What you need
A drum – preferably a Gato or 'Tongue' drum (can be played with any drum or any instrument and is a good way to introduce a 'new' instrument). Cardboard.

## Setting up
Make some cut-out cardboard arrows to show children which direction to pass the instrument around. Gather the children into a circle and sit with them, holding the instrument to be passed around. Place the cut-out arrows on the floor, in front of the children and pointing in a clockwise direction.

## What to do
Introduce the drum as being a magic drum because it can make many different sounds. Show the instrument to the children and make as many sounds as possible on it. Talk about the drum and ask the children questions about it.

Explain that everyone is going to play the drum in turn. Show them how to pass the drum along the line of the arrow to the next child. Pass or give the drum to the child on your left, reciting as you do so the words, 'magic drum, magic drum, play the magic drum!'. Encourage each child to touch the drum and to make a sound on it, praising them as they do so and commenting on the sound that they have made (that was a beautiful sound, it was a very loud sound/ quiet sound. Your sound made me want to dance!).

Encourage children to pass the drum around the circle to the child sitting on their left. If they are unsure about passing it on, take the drum yourself to the next child. Talk about the fact that you are passing it around the circle so that everyone can have a turn at playing.

## Questions to ask

What do you think this is? What is it made of? What does it feel like? Can you pass the drum along the arrow to the next child? What sound can you make? Can you make one sound/lots of sounds? Can the magic drum play a quiet sound? Can you hear your name when I play it ? (Beat the rhythm of the child's name on the drum).

## For younger children
Help younger children to pass the drum along. They might be reticent about playing the drum but let them feel it and tell you something about it. Play their name on the drum for them, telling them that the drum is saying their name and asking them if they can hear it.

## For older children
Older children might need help to pass the drum in the direction of the arrows from right to left. They can be encouraged to explore more sounds and to compare their sound with those of others.

> **Follow-up activities**
> ● Place the drum in the sound area for free exploration.
> ● Tape record some sounds on the Gato drum, play the sounds to the children and ask them to draw the drum while they listen.
> ● Talk about other drums and show pictures or videos of them being played. Show the children real instruments if you can or invite people in to play their instruments. Explore any other drums which you have.

# CHINESE NEW YEAR MUSIC

*Learning objective*
To experience some of the sounds associated with the Chinese New Year.

*Group size*
Four children.

## What you need
Pitched percussion instruments (xylophones, glockenspiels or chime bars), bells, gongs, eight beaters. Pictures showing Chinese New Year celebrations, pictures of the animal associated with the current year, short extract of Chinese music, a tape recorder/ CD player.

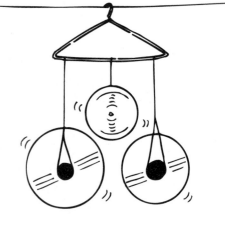

## Setting up
Consult your local library or music shop for some Chinese music or improvise yourself (see below).

Set up two pitched percussion instruments with all of the notes carefully removed except for CDEGA. If you have chime bars select only those five notes. (These notes are often, but not exclusively, used in some traditional Chinese music.) Set out eight beaters and the gongs and bells. Use as many varieties as possible or improvise by suspending saucepan lids. Place all of the instruments on the floor. Set up the tape recorder to one side near to you with the recorded tape loaded. Mount the pictures on the wall in the home area.

## What to do
Start the tape playing as the children come in and gather them together on the carpet. Draw their attention to the pictures and tell them that you are going to another country!

When they have listened for a few moments, stop the tape and ask the children if they can tell you what country you are visiting. Ask them (and explain to them) what is happening in each picture. Ask them if they can tell you which instruments they heard.

Next, move the instruments into the middle of the group and ensure that each child has something to play. Let the children explore the instruments. After one or two minutes, return to the group and listen to what each child is doing. Ask the children to play the gongs and bells. Encourage them to play the pitched instruments by playing one note after another and then by leaving some out and playing them more randomly. Afterwards listen to the music again, and continue to play it on different occasions throughout the week.

## Questions to ask
Which country do you think we are visiting? What can you see in the pictures? Can you hear the bells/gongs in the music?

## For younger children
They will enjoy role playing the actions for gongs and bells.

## For older children
Ask them, for example, to 'announce' the dragon using the gong.

**Follow-up activities**
● Make dragon and animal masks and role play the movements of the animals.
● Taste Chinese food and talk about the ingredients; handle chopsticks.
● Celebrate the Chinese New Year with food, dance, music, costume and role play.

# UNDERWATER MUSIC

*Learning objective*
To understand and care about the environment of sea creatures.

*Group size*
Four to six children.

## What you need
Pictures of sea creatures (dolphins, different species of fish, crabs, starfish, seals and whales), pictures showing litter on the beach and oil in the sea. Taped sea sounds (crashing waves, waves lapping the shore). Taped sounds of dolphins and whales. Instruments or sound makers (shakers, rain makers, tambourines, cymbal). Two containers, one with clean water and one with oily water.

## Setting up
Place the pictures of sea creatures at child height around the area in which you will be working. Set up the tape recorder. Gather the children together and place the instruments to one side.

## What to do
Look at the pictures of the sea creatures, naming them and talking about them. Explain that they all live in the sea, find their food in the sea, play and travel around in the sea. Play the tape of dolphins and whales (one minute short extract) and explain that the sounds are the creatures talking to each other.

Show the children the two containers of water and look at the differences. Tell them that the creatures cannot live in the sea if it is full of oil or very dirty but need clean water to live in. Encourage them to join in with you to role play animals in the sea playing in clean water, swimming freely. Contrast this with the animals being unable to move easily or find food in oily water.

Encourage the children to use the instruments to make sounds to represent the animals in the clear water and those in thick oil and dirt who cannot move easily. Encourage children to talk about the feelings of the animals as they play happily in the clear sea and discuss how the animals must feel in dirty, oily water.

## Questions to ask
(Looking at the pictures.) What is this animal called? Where does he/she live? Where do the animals eat their food? Where do they play and sleep? What happens when they have to try and swim in dirty, oily water? Where do you think the dolphins and whales are happiest? If you were covered in oil and dirt each day would it be very nice?

## For younger children
Talk about the animals and role play them swimming and playing. Ask them to contribute sounds for the whale, fish and dolphin movements and to notice the difference between clear and dirty water.

## For older children
Encourage older children to develop more observations about the differences between clean and dirty water. Develop their manipulative skills in controlling the instruments to make a variety of sounds.

**Follow-up activities**
● Make models and draw pictures of sea creatures. Colour and cut out fish shapes to make a mobile.
● Move around to sea creature music (whale and dolphin sounds) exploring the movements of crabs, fish, seals, starfish, jelly fish.
● Look at dirty ponds and puddles and clean water. Collect samples of each in containers and talk about them.

# NOMADS

*Learning objective*
To understand that
people live in different
ways and in different
places.

*Group size*
Four to eight.

## What you need
Pictures of nomadic peoples in the desert (showing camels,
clothes and tents), pictures of the desert, sand dunes and
an oasis. A selection of instruments and sound makers
with which the children are familiar.

## Setting up
Make up a story about a little Arab boy called Odeh who lives in
the desert. Include the idea of a 'moving house', sleeping in a tent
each night in a different place, the need for the camels to carry the
loads, the need to wear flowing, long clothing covering their heads
and the need to find an oasis for water. Keep the story short! Mount
the pictures on card and stand them on the floor at the front of the
area. Put the instruments in a group in front of you and gather the
children around, sitting on the floor.

## What to do
Look at the pictures together and talk about them. Encourage the
children to tell you about things which they notice and to answer
questions. Tell them the story of Odeh, the little boy in the desert.
Ensure that they remain still and quiet whilst you are telling the story.

Next ask the children to suggest and make sounds by coming into
the middle and playing the instruments. Pick out a few points in the
story where they can add sounds (walking along in the desert, feeling
very hot and tired, riding on a camel, sounds for the water in the
oasis and for the sand as he walks along, going to sleep in the tent,
waking up to the hot sun in the morning). Talk about these points
with the children and then tell the story slowly again, explaining
that they are going to add sounds to the story.

## Questions to ask
What can you see in the pictures? What is that animal? Have you
seen a camel? Is it raining? Does it look hot? What sort of home do
the people live in? Have you been in a tent? Tell me about the animal's
back. Where do the people get their water from? Does it come out of
a tap? How do they carry water across the desert? What trees grow in
the desert?

## For younger children
If the whole group is made up of younger children, shorten the story
and encourage them to make sounds at one or two points.

## For older children
Ask older children to contribute more ideas and to suggest sounds for
a number of points in the story. Build up the number of sounds
gradually. Repeat the story while doing this and encourage the
children to memorize where the sounds fit into the story.

### Follow-up activities
● Role play dressing
up in flowing robes
and headgear,
carrying water and
living in a tent. (Set
up a tent if you can).
● Make models and
tell the story in the
sand area, with
dunes, an oasis,
tents, camels and
people. Trace the
outline of the camel's
hump in the sand.
● Cut out camel
shapes, colour them
in or add collage
materials. Make a
display of a camel
train in a frieze with a
background of tents
and an oasis.

CHAPTER FOUR

*Help children explore, identify and recognize sounds in their environment as an integral part of understanding how things work, with these activities which involve children in listening to objects in the made and natural world. Other activities will encourage them to understand how their own bodies function.*

# SOUND WALK

*Learning objective*
To identify features of the natural and made world by listening to sounds.

*Group size*
Eight to ten children.

## What you need
Pictures of any of the features which you might encounter on a local walk (birds, trees), battery tape recorder with inbuilt microphone and blank cassette, adult helpers.

## Setting up
Decide on a suitable walk (playground, park, wood) and obtain any necessary permissions to take the children out. Survey the walk area for particular features of interest and to note any hazards. Ensure that children have the correct clothing and there are sufficient adults.

## What to do
Talk to the children about where you will be going on your walk and ask them to suggest things that they might see or hear. Look at pictures of people, animals, natural/made objects which you might encounter.

Take the children to the location and listen to the sounds around you. Ask them to tell you what sounds they can hear. From time to time, gather the children together and ask them to be very quiet so that you can record a sound. Collect any small objects of interest on the walk (fallen leaves, conkers).

When you are back in the nursery, play back the tape and listen to the sounds. Talk about what you heard on your walk, name them and remember the features.

## Questions to ask
What can you hear? Can you be very quiet and still? Can you hear any small things moving? Can you hear any cars or large animals? What do you think is making that sound? Where do you think the sound is coming from? Do you think the sound (name it) is very near to us? Is it a long way away? How do you know?

## For younger children
Visit somewhere close by. Encourage them to talk about the features you encounter and to name them, perhaps recording only two sounds for play back.

## For older children
Older children will be able to show their understanding of more features which they encounter and will be able to name them. See if they can identify some sounds as being near or far away.

---

**Follow-up activities**
● Paint an object found on the sound walk and explore what sounds can be made with it.
● Record a sound and learn how to play it back.
● Draw pictures to match a sound.
● Tape record different locations.

---

# TRAVELLING TOYS

*Learning objective*
To understand why
toys make different
sounds moving on
different surfaces.

*Group size*
Four children.

## What you need
A variety of small (toy cars) and large (sit-on) movable toys with wheels, made of different materials (rubber or wooden wheels). Two surfaces to move them on (carpet and smooth shiny surface such as a tiled floor, card or table top).

## Setting up
Gather the toys together and ensure that there are two different surfaces for the children to use.

## What to do
Explain that you are all going to listen to some toys as they are moved on the carpet and on the smooth surface. Ask the children to notice the different sounds that each toy makes. Start with small toys (such as small cars) first one and then two on the same and then different surfaces. Select pairs of toys with contrasting characteristics to try out. Next, take a large toy on which children can sit and ask them to move it along on the carpet and on the smooth floor. Encourage the children to make loud and quiet sounds with their voices as they move along.

Develop the children's language skills by asking them to tell you about their observations. Encourage them to feel the two surfaces and to describe them. Through questioning encourage understanding of loud and quiet in relation to the two different surfaces and the sound made by the material of the wheels.

## Questions to ask
Do these wheels make a quiet/loud sound? Why does this toy make a quiet sound as it moves along? What are the wheels made of? Can you feel them and tell me about them? Can you make a quiet/loud sound with your voices? (Demonstrate.) Can you join in with me?

## For younger children
Younger children will be able to notice the difference in sound and to tell you which is quiet and which is loud. They might not want to contribute a voice sound but can listen to the other children's contributions and might be encouraged to join in. Let them play with one toy to begin with and then encourage them to try a contrasting toy. If they simply want to play in their own space, try to encourage the language and understanding of quiet and loud.

## For older children
Encourage older children to consider more contrasts, assessing the toys on the same and different surfaces. They will more readily contribute sounds of their own but still might need to be encouraged to join in with you.

**Follow-up activities**
● Play loud and quiet sounds on sound makers and instruments.
● Look at trains, cars, tractors and talk about what their wheels are made of.
● Tape record the sounds of small toys moving on different surfaces.

# SHAKING GRAINS

**Learning objective**
*To understand that different materials make different sounds inside containers.*

**Group size**
*Two to four children.*

## What you need
Containers (yoghurt pots, small cartons, plastic bottles with screw tops) and a selection of materials to put inside and shake (pasta, rice, peas, sugar). Make sure that some of the containers have lids which are sealed and some have tops which lift off or unscrew. Some of the containers can be opaque and some transparent. A small bowl of each material.

## Setting up
Gather the children around the containers and materials.

## What to do
Start by looking at three or four of the materials and encourage the children to look at them and touch them. Question the children about the names of the materials and ask them to talk about how they are used.

Put some of each material in turn into an identical container and shake the contents, encouraging the children to talk about the different sounds. Next, shake some of the opaque containers and let the children guess what is inside by listening to the sound. When they have tried to guess let them tip out the contents to see if they were right.

## Questions to ask
How does this pasta feel? What does it look like? Do you eat/ like pasta? Can you shake it quickly and slowly? Can you shake your hands while I shake the pasta? What do you think is inside? Does it sound the same as this? Can you take the top off and tell me what is inside?

## For younger children
Let them explore the materials and containers, telling you about their observations. They will find it easier to use the transparent containers for recognition but might want to shake the containers in a random fashion. Encourage them to name the materials.

## For older children
Older children can be encouraged to try out different materials in the containers and will be able to distinguish more of the contents of the opaque containers.

**Follow-up activities**
● Make individual shakers and decorate them.
● Play the shakers while singing a song, rhyme, or in a sound story.
● Try whole body movements while you shake the containers slowly or quickly.

# MICROPHONE GAME

*Learning objective*
*To understand that sounds can be amplified electronically.*

*Group size*
*Eight to ten children.*

## What you need
Pictures of singers using a microphone, a microphone and stand, an amplification unit or tape recorder with amplifier. If you do not have access to this equipment, role play the activity using junk materials.

## Setting up
Many primary and secondary schools have a PA system; perhaps older pupils could help you carry out the activity. Place the microphone on a stand at the front of the group. CARE! Ensure that the microphone is connected to the amplification system. If role playing the activity improvise a stand and microphone using junk materials. Set up the pictures at child height.

## What to do
Gather the children around. Look at the pictures and encourage them to name and use the word microphone. Ask them to listen carefully to you speaking or singing with and without the microphone. Question the children about any differences that they notice. Ask the children one by one to come out and speak their name into the microphone. If any child is reluctant to do so, then speak their name for them.

Encourage all the children to develop confidence in using the microphone with your support.

## Questions to ask
Do you know what this is called? What do we use it for? Can you listen to me speaking into it or singing? Is it the same when I speak without using the microphone? Can you come and speak your name into it?

## For younger children
Younger children will notice the differences but might not want to say their name into it. Encourage them by making lots of sounds yourself and setting up a fun atmosphere.

## For older children
Older children might be unstoppable in this activity! Once they have gained confidence in speaking their name, let them try some songs or rhymes.

**Follow-up activities**
● Talk about where you would use a microphone.
● Encourage children to role play their favourite pop or television star, while speaking or singing.
● Make loud and quiet sounds on an instrument.
● Paint pictures of favourite pop or television stars.

# WATER MUSIC

**Learning objective**
To observe and
understand what
happens when air is
blown into water.

**Group size**
Two to four children.

## What you need
Drinking straws, small beakers, bowls, water, table tennis balls.

## Setting up
Collect the children around the water area and ensure that their sleeves are rolled up and they are wearing overalls or aprons.

## What to do
Blow down a straw onto the water without immersing the straw. Ask the children what they can see and hear. Blow down a straw onto each child's hand and encourage them to tell you what it feels like. Give each child a straw and let them explore the sensation of blowing onto their own hands. Ask the children to role play making quiet sounds for a soft breeze by blowing through their mouths.

Next encourage them to blow softly on the water to move floating table tennis balls; ask them to tell you what happens. Now show them what happens when the straw is immersed as you blow down it. Encourage the children to observe what happens and to describe the water each time.

Fill a bowl of water or a beaker for each child and let them blow down the straw into the water. Ask them to describe what the water looks like when it is still and when air is being blown into it.

## Questions to ask
(Without the straw.) Can you breath in? Show me how you breath out. (Demonstrate.) What do we breath? Can you feel the air on your hand? (With the straw.) Can you blow softly onto the water? What does the water look like when you do this? Can you make the sound of a very quiet wind? What do you see when you put the straw into the water and then blow down it? Can you make the sound of bubbles with your lips and mouths? (Demonstrate.)

## For younger children
Younger children will enjoy making the bubbles but might not be able to control gentle blowing especially with the table tennis balls on the water. Encourage them to blow onto their hands instead and to tell you what it feels like.

## For older children
Older children will be able to control their blowing more easily and can try to make the balls move faster and slower across the water.

**Follow-up activities**
● Try blowing gently into a small paper bag and observe what happens.
● Make a collage using bubble wrap and smooth Cellophane paper.
● Move around shaking and jumping like bubbles.
● Listen to a tape recording of a kettle boiling.

# BODY PERCUSSION

*Learning objective*
*To understand how parts of the body work by listening to body sounds and making actions.*

*Group size*
*Four to six children.*

## What you need
Pictures of parts of the body (hands, feet, fingers, teeth), pictures of children making sounds (clapping, stamping), songs and rhymes which use body sounds and actions.

## Setting up
Practise making sounds yourself with different parts of the body – knuckles, finger nails, fingers rubbed together, hands patting chest, stomach, thighs, clapping, feet sliding, tapping and stamping. Gather children together in a small group with the pictures on a wall nearby or on a table.

## What to do
Talk with the children about the pictures, asking them to identify parts of the body. Start with one part of the body and explore the sounds and actions it can make. Make actions and sounds yourself for each part of the body and encourage the children to copy.

Encourage them to contribute their own sounds and actions and involve the whole group in imitating each other's suggestions. Instigate discussion about the functions of different parts of the body, role playing what feet, hands and so on help us to do.

## Questions to ask
What do we call this part of our body? Can you make this sound? (Demonstrate.) Can you make another sound with your hands? What do we use our hands for? Which sound do you like making? Is this a loud sound or a quiet sound? Can you make a very quiet sound with your feet? When do you have to walk very quietly? Can you walk very quietly around the table?

## For younger children
Younger children will find the larger movements easier to copy but they might not offer any suggestions themselves. Encourage them to name the parts of the body and to make the sounds that you suggest.

## For older children
Older children will be able to control smaller movements and will observe the differences in sound such as whole hand compared with a two finger clap. They will probably find it easier to contribute their own suggestions. Once the children are able to show you a number of sounds, ask them to choose three different sounds and to play them one after the other.

---

**Follow-up activities**
● Make hand and foot prints, tape record hand and foot sounds and place the tape near to the prints.
● Collect pictures of hands which have different skin colours and belong to different-aged people. Encourage children to talk about the differences.

# TOWN SOUNDS

*Learning objective*
*To understand the functions of various features in the built environment*

*Group size*
*Four to six children.*

## What you need
Photocopiable page 62, pictures of buildings in your area (school, supermarket).

## Setting up
Collect the children into a small group in the home corner and give them each a copy of photocopiable page 62. Display pictures of local buildings.

## What to do
Look at the photocopied sheet with the children and encourage them to explore it, telling you which features they can recognize. Concentrate then on one particular feature, such as the supermarket, and encourage language about what happens there, making sounds associated with it (trolleys moving fast and slow, tills at the check out, people talking, tannoy announcements, money rattling). Encourage children to contribute comment and appropriate sounds for each area on the map, involving movement where possible and role playing where appropriate to encourage imagination.

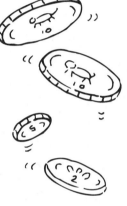

## Questions to ask
Have you been to the (supermarket)? What sounds can you hear there? Is it a very quiet place? What do people do there? Can you push the trolley fast, slow? (Role play.) What sound does it make? Why do we go to the (hospital)?

## For younger children
Focus on one feature of the 'town', choose one with which they will all be familiar, such as the supermarket, and encourage them to role play. They might find it difficult to suggest sounds but these will gradually emerge from role play and questioning.

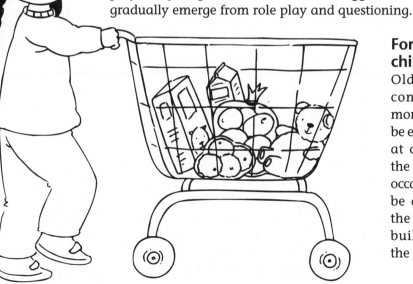

## For older children
Older children will contribute sounds more easily and can be encouraged to look at different parts of the town on different occasions. They might be able to sequence the sounds within a building or around the whole town.

## Follow-up activities
● Set up the home area as one of the buildings and role play what happens inside.
● Paint pictures of one feature of the town and make a frieze of different buildings.
● Compose a tape which includes children's contributions for each building on the frieze.

# TOWER BLOCKS

*Learning objective*
*To begin to notice*
*differences between*
*high and low in space*
*and sound.*

*Group size*
*Two to four children.*

## What you need
Building blocks, pictures of high and low buildings, small pitched percussion instruments xylophones, glockenspiels and beaters.

## Setting up
Gather the children around a table with some building blocks in front of each child. Display the pictures nearby or have them on the table with you. Put the xylophones, glockenspiels and beaters on a table by you.

## What to do.
Encourage children to place the blocks on top of each other and to see how high they can make a tower. Show them that the building might be less wobbly and more secure if it has more bricks on the base. Look at the pictures of very high buildings.

Next, hold the small xylophone up vertically and play the instrument by moving the beaters from bottom to top while telling them about a lift which is going up in the building. Ask them to try to make their building blocks go higher while they listen to the lift going up.

## Questions to ask
Can you put the bricks on top of each other? Can you make a high building with your bricks? Can you build the bricks up while I move the lift up? (Playing the xylophone with a beater moving from low notes to high.) Can you show me the high building?

## For younger children
Younger children will still be at the stage of trying to balance bricks. They can look at the pictures and be encouraged to notice the difference between high and low buildings. They can listen to the 'lift' and pretend to be the lift going higher as the sound gets higher.

## For older children
Older children will have better manipulative skills and will be able to build higher buildings; they will often understand the idea of the need for a secure base most easily. Encourage them to grasp the idea of a lift going up and coming down and encourage them to role play the lift in sound, moving up and down the xylophone with the beaters from a low sound to a high sound. They might not be able to easily distinguish high and low in sound and so their sounds might be rather haphazard.

### Follow-up activities
● Move whole bodies, arms and hands from high to low while role playing a story (someone climbing up the stairs, Jack and the Beanstalk).
● Make high and low buildings using junk materials and other construction materials.
● Sing and play action songs and rhymes which encourage understanding of high and low.

CHAPTER FIVE

*Develop the children's manipulative skills by holding, using and playing a variety of musical instruments and by controlling vocal, body and electronic sounds. Encourage them to climb, stop, start, travel quickly or slowly in response to musical elements and recorded music, encountering a variety of apparatus.*

# ACTION SOUNDS

**Learning objective**
*To role play the actions involved in handling equipment and tools.*

**Group size**
*Eight to ten children.*

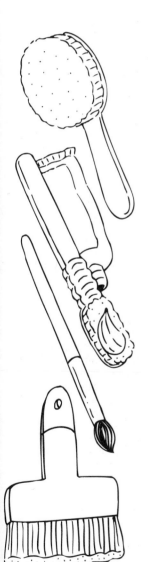

## What you need
A tape recording of sounds made by hammering, sweeping, pouring, cutting, mixing; the same actions at both slow and fast speeds.

## Setting up
Use a large space. Set up the tape recorder on a table. (CARE!)

## What to do
Seat the children around you on the floor and explain to them that you are going to think about the actions involved in working about the house: hammering, cutting, sweeping, pouring, mixing and sawing. Ask individual children if they can show you the actions required for each task and encourage them all to join in. Discuss what tools and equipment are required to do the jobs.

Next ask the children to stand up and spread out. Help the children to find a space and then ask them to stand still. Tell them that you are going to play a sound and they have to guess what action to do. Explain that you do not want them to call out or put their hands up but to show you the movement.

Take each sound in turn and encourage the children to make the actions. Praise their efforts and ask the children to watch each other. When they are quite happy with all of the actions, encourage them to move their whole bodies in movements for actions such as hammering, sweeping and sawing.

## Questions to ask
What can you cut a piece of paper with? Show me with your fingers how the scissors work. (Demonstrate yourself.) Can you show me how to saw? Can you sweep with a large broom, a small brush? Show me how to hammer in a small nail/a big fence post?

## For younger children
Concentrate on one action for each sound. Start with the gross motor movements and progress to the fine movements such as cutting. Ensure that they can recognize some of the sounds on the tape.

## For older children
Encourage them to try out the different ways of hammering, sweeping and so on, considering what equipment is being used. Try to sequence the actions, and to copy each other making fast and slow actions.

**Follow-up activities**
● Using the photocopiable sheet on page 63, ask the children to make up some sounds for the actions. Encourage them to make vocal sounds (demonstrate yourself) or to use instruments, for instance a shaker moved slowly for brushing, a metal brush moved quickly across a guiro for sawing.
● Draw pictures of a hammer, saw, scissors, broom, spoon and bowl, jug.
● Collect different brushes (a broom, hand brush and pan, toothbrush, paint brush, hairbrush, dog/cat brush and a baby's brush) and talk about what they are used for, making the actions for each.

# FIREWORKS

*Learning objective*
*To explore the*
*movements of*
*fireworks using the*
*whole body.*

*Group size*
*Four to eight children.*

## What you need
A large space, an adult helper, tape recording of different fireworks, tape recording of 'Fireworks' by Igor Stravinsky, tape recorder.

## Setting up
Practise making vocal sounds such as 'Whoosh', 'Bang', 'Zipp', 'Screech', 'Whee!' yourself until you feel confident. Set up the tape recorder.(CARE!) Switch on and load the firework sound tape.

## What to do
Help the children to spread out in the space and explain to them that they are going to pretend to be fireworks. Select a well known firework to begin with such as a rocket and listen to the sound of it taking off. Ask the children to crouch down low on the floor, then to shoot up in the air with their whole bodies, pushing their arms up high. Talk about where the firework goes and what happens after it has shot upwards. Explain that the stick falls back to the ground when the firework is finished and the children can fall back on the floor when they have stretched up as high as possible.

Explore a few different fireworks in this way, drawing attention to particular children and praising them all separately. Individual children will need to be encouraged in different ways. Observe carefully and help all of them to explore a range of movements. When you have tried all of the fireworks on the tape, ask the children to sit down and be very quiet while they rest for a moment.

Now play a short extract from 'Fireworks' by Stravinsky. Ask the children to think about the firework sounds as they listen. If they are restless stop the tape and calm them.

Next, help them to spread out again, tell them that you will play the music again and this time you would like them to pretend to be fireworks and move around the space. Some children will find this difficult and will need encouragement.

## Questions to ask
Can you show me how a rocket moves? Can you crouch down on the floor and shoot up quickly? Can you stretch up really high? What does a Catherine wheel do? Can you move your arm around in a circle? (Demonstrate.) Can you spin around with your whole body?

## For younger children
Concentrate on one or two fireworks and think of, or imitate a movement that goes with each.

## For older children
Encourage them to think about the beginning and end of the firework movements, to control a wider range of movements and to move through a sequence.

**Follow-up activities**
● Ask children to hold hands to make a circle and to move slowly as a group pretending to be a large Catherine wheel. Explore the movements needed with feet and legs in order to go faster, but do not spend too long going fast as the children will become dizzy!
● Join children together in a long line and pretend to be a rocket taking off across the hall. Practise this slowly at first.
● Make firework music with the 'Musical Fireworks' activity on page 53.

# RAILWAY STATIONS

*Learning objective*
To travel with other children in a line at different speeds around a track.

*Group size*
Six to eight children; possibly larger groups once familiar.

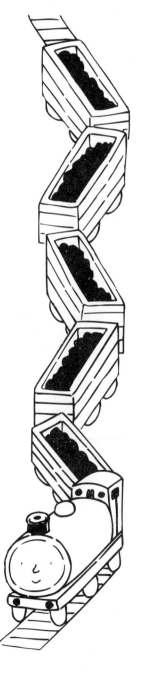

## What you need
A large space, large cards labelled with stations (use stations near to your locality), long length of coloured string or paper (chalk if outside), long pieces of card to indicate the tunnels, steep hill, level crossing and (red) stop/(green) start signs. A selection of percussion instruments.

## Setting up
Lay out the coloured string, paper or chalk for the railway track. Leave enough space between the two sides for children to move in between as the train.

## What to do
Gather the children into the large space and tell them that they will be playing a train game. Show them the lines for the track and demonstrate how they will have to move inside them. Help individual children to stand inside the track and ask them to move very slowly around it. Next, with one adult at the head and another at the end, ask the children to put their hands on each other's waists and move slowly around the track in a line. Next try to move a little faster.

When this has been achieved, explain that you are now going to put in some other features. Place the signs for the tunnel, hill, level crossing and the stations in position together. Explain that the train slows down as it approaches the station and gets faster as it leaves.

Select two children to be the train and help them to travel round the track while the others watch. Remind them to slow down for the stations and other features. Next, help all of the children to form the train again and with two adults travel round the track.

Encourage the children to make train sounds as the train moves along, demonstrate yourself and ask them to join in. Ask two children to sit in the middle and beat a tambourine as the train moves along.

## Questions to ask
Can you travel slowly, quickly around the track? Can you tell me which station this is? What happens to the train as it gets near to the stations? Does anyone know what happens at a level crossing? Will it go faster or slower up the hill? What sound does the train make as it enters a tunnel or comes near to a level crossing?

## For younger children
Leave out the tunnel, hill, level crossing and stop/start. Concentrate on moving around singly and in pairs and then in a line, going slow and fast and progressing to slowing down and getting faster.

## For older children
Encourage them to make the vocal sounds for the train as it goes along, whistles, goes over a level crossing and through a tunnel as well as making the slow, fast, slower and faster movements.

**Follow-up activities**
● Place children together with instruments at the different places on the track and encourage them to make sounds as the train reaches each station, goes through the tunnel or over the crossing.
● Recite the poem, 'The Engine Driver' by Clive Sansom (in 'Language and Literacy', *Learning in the Early Years*, Scholastic) and make the rhythm of the train to fit in with the syllables of jic/ket/ty can. Use hands, tambour, tambourine or metal guiro.
● Listen to the music, 'Coronation Scot' by Vivian Ellis or 'Puffing Billy' by Edward White. Move around imaginatively.

# COPY CAT

**Learning objective**
To develop fine motor movements and manipulative skills using small instruments.

**Group size**
Two to four children.

## What you need
A range of small instruments (tambourine, maracas, guiros, rainmaker, shakers) or child-made instruments and sound sources of different sizes.

## Setting up
Place the instruments in the middle of a small space.

## What to do
Gather the children around and explain that you are going to play some of the instruments. Start with the shakers: first shake your wrists and ask the children if they can do the same. Ask them to show you 'still wrists' and 'shaking wrists'. Next, take one of the shakers and ask them to tell you what happens to the sound when your wrists are still/shaking. Pass a shaken instrument to each child and ask them to copy you, first making no sound and then shaking the instrument. Next, while saying the words, 'shake, still', ask the children to make up their own sounds and pattern.

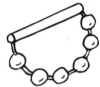

Once the children can do this, select another instrument, for instance the tambourine, and show them how to shake it, placing their hand around the wooden or plastic rim and putting their thumb in the hole. If you have a rainmaker show the children how to control the instrument. Encourage them to listen to the sound when it is moved to a vertical position suddenly or gradually. If they have child-made shakers and instruments, encourage the children to control the sounds by shaking them quickly and slowly. Try the other shaken instruments, such as maraccas and bells or jingle sticks. Encourage control by listening to the sound.

## Questions to ask
Where are your wrists? Can you shake them/keep them still? Can you hold the instrument very still? Now can you shake it? Can you shake it very quickly/very slowly? What happens when you tip the rain maker up? Can you make fast/slow rain? Can you shake your wrists when I shake the tambourine?

## For younger children
Concentrate on developing fine motor skills with each instrument in turn. Give them the easiest instruments to hold at first, for instance the small hand jingle or jingle stick. Progress to the maraccas, tubo shaker and tambourine.

## For older children
Older children can be encouraged to make fast and slow sounds and to manipulate and control the more difficult instruments such as the rainmaker, making slow sounds on it. They can be encouraged to make up their own patterns of sound and silence (shaken/still).

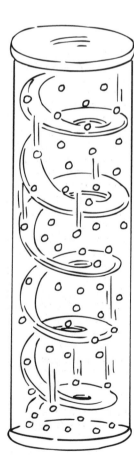

**Follow-up activities**
● Shake different parts of the body in turn and learn to control them. Give cues to the children by shaking a tambourine when you want them to shake.
● Make patterns with 'wiggly' lines, moving from left to right and leaving blank spaces for the silence. Show the children how to 'play' the music and ask them to make up their own patterns and play them.
● Chalk a wiggly, shaky line outside in the playground, interspersed with gaps and ask the children to move along the line, shaking their whole bodies while they are on it and not shaking while they travel across the space in between the lines. Add sounds to this, remaining silent while travelling across the gaps.

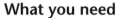

# CIRCUS

**Learning objective**
*To develop the skills of balancing and climbing while moving imaginatively.*

**Group size**
*Six to eight children.*

## What you need
Another adult helper, pictures of people performing circus acts (tightrope walker, trapeze artist, clowns) – do not include pictures of animals in the circus. A range of floor blocks or low, broad-based equipment which can bear the weight of children, a large space, climbing apparatus, tambourine.

## Setting up
Mount the pictures on boards or at child height at the front. Lay out the floor blocks leaving plenty of space in between them and within reach of, but not too close to, of the climbing apparatus. Help the children to change into suitable clothing and footwear.

## What to do
Look at the pictures of the circus acts and talk about what is happening in each one. Explain how the trapeze artist has to climb to the top of the big top tent, how he swings on a rope and how he balances on a wire. Ask the children if they have seen a circus and ask them if they can remember anything about the people.

Next, help them to move into a space and encourage them to role play the actions for climbing, balancing and swinging. When they have done this, help each in turn to stand on a low floor block and balance, remaining still.

Now all pretend to be on the high trapeze wire and, to create atmosphere, shake the tambourine. Ask the children to try balancing by holding their arms out on either side and also by dropping their arms by their sides. Explain that they must jump off when you strike the tambourine.

Next explain that you want them to climb as high as they can on the apparatus and then to come down again. Station one adult at the climbing apparatus and one at the floor blocks. Ensure that every child uses the floor blocks and attempts to use the climbing apparatus.

## Questions to ask
Have you been to a circus or seen one on the television? What did you see people doing? What is this person doing in the picture? Can you climb onto the floor block? Can you stand very still? How high can you climb? Can you climb onto the first step/right up to the top?

## For younger children
Concentrate on using the floor blocks and developing their control of balancing and jumping off by listening to the tambourine.

## For older children
Older children can be encouraged to balance in a variety of ways and to sequence the movements by climbing up, down, balancing and jumping off. They can be encouraged to climb higher.

**Follow-up activities**
● Encourage imaginative movement as the children listen to 'Circus Polka' by Igor Stravinsky. Encourage actions for climbing, running, tumbling and juggling.
● Paint pictures of circus artists such as clowns, using crayons, pastels or collage materials and mount them on a frieze.
● Talk about the conditions which elephants and lions need for living. Explain that they cannot have these conditions in the circus. Make up a story about a lion kept in a circus and how he feels when he is set free.

# CARNIVAL OF THE ANIMALS

*Learning objective*
To respond to recorded music by moving imaginatively.

*Group size*
Six to ten children.

## What you need
A large space, tape recorder or CD player, recording of 'Carnival of the Animals' by Camille Saint-Saëns, 'The elephant' and 'Kangaroos'. Pictures of kangaroos and elephants.

## Setting up
Listen to the recording beforehand and locate the correct tracks. Have the tape/CD ready.

## What to do
Seat the children on the floor in front of you and look at the pictures of the kangaroos and elephants together. Talk about the animals, encouraging the children to contribute from their own knowledge. Draw attention to the huge size, heavy weight and long trunk of the elephant and to the jumps and leaps that a kangaroo can make.

Play the track, 'The elephant' and ask the children to think about what it sounds like the animal is doing. Explain that they are going to pretend to be the elephant. Encourage their imagination by asking questions.

Help all the children to move into a space, play 'The elephant' again and ask them to move around like an elephant. Praise the children's efforts. When that track has finished, ask the children to sit down again and listen to the music for 'Kangaroos'. Ask them to listen for jumps in the music and to imagine the kangaroo jumping. After they have listened to this, ask one or two children to show you how they can jump like a kangaroo. Praise their efforts.

Explain that you are going to play 'Kangaroos' again and that this time the children can move around, jumping from a crouching position. Value and praise all of their efforts but also encourage them to extend their movements, jumping further and higher.

## Questions to ask
Do you know which animal this is? (Looking at the picture.) What do you know about him? What is this long piece of his body called? What does he use his trunk for? What does he do with his ears? Is he a large/small animal? Are his feet large or small?

## For younger children
Encourage younger children to name the animals and to tell you about them. Help them with a few ideas for movement if they cannot think of anything and concentrate on the jumping kangaroo.

## For older children
Older children can be encouraged to think about a few movements for each animal and to move while listening to both tracks. Try a variety of movements for each animal, thinking about how they walk, eat their food and so on.

### Follow-up activities
● Crayon, paint or use pastels to make pictures of kangaroos and elephants. Stick on a piece of material for the kangaroos pouch, draw a small baby kangaroo and place it inside of the pouch; add large ears and a trunk made from material on to an outline of an elephant.
● Make jumping sounds using instruments such as a wooden agogo.
● Listen to an adult play a flexitone (borrow one from your local primary or secondary school). Find very low sounds on the keyboard to represent the elephant.

# FAST AND SLOW

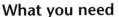

**Learning objective**
*To develop co-ordination at fast and slow speeds.*

**Group size**
*Four to eight children.*

## What you need
Tape recorder or CD player, two or three different percussion instruments or a keyboard, picture of a swan, recordings of pieces of music which have fast or slow sections. Such as: (fast) ' William Tell Overture' by Gioachino Rossini (last section beginning with a trumpet fanfare); (slow) 'The swan' from 'The Carnival of the Animals'. This activity will need to take place in stages over a period of time.

## Setting up
Set up the tape recorder or CD player.

## What to do
Seat the children in a circle. Play some fast sounds on an instrument (play single sounds very quickly, one after the other). Ask the children to tell you about the sounds and explain that the sounds are fast. Ask one child to leave his/her place in the circle and move at a fast speed around the outside, returning to, and sitting down in his place. Encourage the rest of the group to pat quickly on their legs.

Tell the children that you are going to listen to some fast music. Play a section of the 'William Tell Overture'. To channel the children's energy and to help them concentrate on the music, ask them to pretend to be riding a horse by making galloping movements with their hands and arms.

Next play some slow sounds on an instrument (one sound after another, moving slowly with spaces between the sounds). Ask the children to tell you about the sounds and explain that you are playing them slowly. Ask one child to walk around the circle very slowly and encourage the others to make slow hand pats on their legs.

Now listen to some very slow music and play 'The swan' from 'Carnival of the Animals'. Ask them to look at the picture of the swan and to think about her gliding along on the water. Play a short section of this and then show them how to make a swan's neck with their hands and arms and to move them slowly around.

## Questions to ask
Can you tell me anything about these sounds? Are they fast or slow sounds? Can you imagine the swan moving very slowly and gliding across the water?

## For younger children
Young children might not be able to co-ordinate fast pats on their legs. Encourage them to make the galloping movements instead with their hands as if they are a rider holding the reins on a horse.

## For older children
Once they can do fast and slow movements successfully, get them to change from slow to fast movements, then fast and back to slow.

**Follow-up activities**
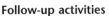
● Make up fast and slow music on two or three instruments placed in the sound area; make labels for fast and slow.
● Move large toys across the floor at fast and slow speeds.
● Collect information and pictures from one of the Wild Fowl Trusts, adopt a swan and follow his progress.

# TOY ROBOT

**Learning objective**
*To make short sharp movements using different parts of the body.*

**Group size**
*Ten to 12 children.*

## What you need
Another adult, large space, metal instruments such as metal agogo or a metal sound source on which you can make short, sharp sounds, hard wooden or metallic beater, recording of electronic jerky sounds or a keyboard, tape recorder/CD player, picture of a toy robot or a short clip of video showing a robot.

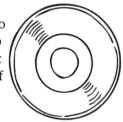

## Setting up
Ensure that you are confident in making short sharp sounds on the metal agogo and that you can find a suitable sound on the keyboard. Set up the tape recorder at the front (CARE!) and load the tape. Place the metal instrument and beater beside you. Set up the keyboard.

## What to do
Seat the children on the floor in a semi circle with plenty of space between each child. Look at the pictures or your drawings of a toy robot and talk about how it moves and how it works. Play some short, sharp sounds on the agogo or other percussion instrument and ask the other adult to pretend to be the robot, moving one part of the body at a time in stiff movements, using head, legs, arms and fingers. Ask the children to join in using their arms. Praise the children's efforts. When they have mastered the arm movements, play some more short sounds and ask them to move their heads. Progress to different parts of the body and eventually to moving along with the whole body.

Listen to a short extract of electronic, jerky sounds or make them yourself on the keyboard. Ask the children to move around the area after they have heard the sounds once, thinking about the movements and actions of a toy robot.

## Questions to ask
Can you tell me about this picture (of the robot)? Do you know what we call it? Can you tell me what it does and how it works? What does it look like? What is it made of? Can you move your arm in sharp, stiff movements? Copy me! Can you try to move your arm when I make the sounds? Show me how you can move your legs as I play the (electronic) sounds.

## For younger children
Encourage them to use their hands and arms for robot movements while remaining stationary. Try making short sharp movements; they may not be able to make them at the same time as the sounds.

## For older children
Develop short, sharp, jerky movement by using more parts of the body, while remaining still and while travelling around. Involve them in an imaginary sequence: switch on, start up, move around, slow up and wind down, switch off.

**Follow-up activities**
● Make models of robots from junk materials.
● Speak like a robot using short, sharp voice sounds and record them.
● Encourage them to say their names like a robot: take the register using robot voices.
● Make up music for robots with a variety of instruments making short, sharp, jerky sounds.

# CREATIVE DEVELOPMENT

## CHAPTER SIX

*The musical activities in this chapter encourage children to explore the feel, sight and sound of natural objects and materials. Link vocal, body and environmental sounds together with child-made, acoustic and electronic instruments, using dance, role play and art to encourage the children's creative skills.*

# SOUND COLLAGE

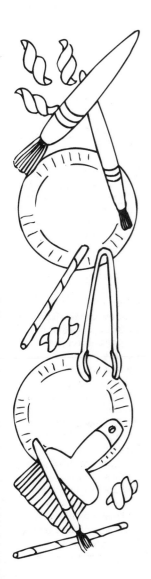

### What you need
A selection of different types of paper, corrugated cardboard, tissue paper, foil, newspaper, Cellophane, pasta shapes and other suitable junk material. Paste, spreaders, large sheets of frieze paper or paper plates.

**Learning objective**
To explore the sound and texture of different materials.

**Group size**
Two to four children.

### Setting up
Cover a table with newspaper and place a selection of the materials in the middle together with the paste and paste brushes. Place the paper plates or the frieze paper nearby.

### What to do
Explore the materials with the children encouraging them to touch and talk about them. Ask them to rustle or scrunch the papers and to listen to the sounds that are made. After a period of exploration, ask them to each choose three materials. Show them how to stick their chosen materials to the paper or plate, encouraging them to move the materials around on the paper and to choose which arrangement they like best.

When completed, mount the plates or frieze paper at child height on the wall for the children to touch.

### Questions to ask
Find a piece that you like: can you tell me about it? Is it rough, smooth, shiny, knobbly? Can you show me the sound it makes? (Hide a piece under the table.) Can you tell me which paper makes this sound? Do you like this paper? Which one do you like? Can you make different patterns with your three materials? Can you move the shapes around?

### For younger children
Younger children can explore the materials and choose one or two that they like. They may need help to paste/stick the materials but they can indicate where they would like them to go.

### For older children
Older children can work together to contribute to one large sheet of frieze paper or select more materials and move them around into different positions before sticking them. Encourage them to find many different sounds from one material (paper brushed, ripped, screwed up, flapped).

**Follow-up activities**
● Explore the completed collage with hands and then with a selection of 'beaters' (brushes, sticks, twigs, straws). 'Play the music' on the wall collage, observing the different sounds made by materials and 'beaters'.
● Encourage children to choose one material and, standing in a line, to each play one sound in sequence, one after the other.
● Using junk material in three dimension, create fantasy creatures and cover the surfaces with different textures and materials.
● Play and tape record the sound of the fantasy creature.

# KEYBOARD SOUNDS

*Learning objective*
*To explore different sounds on the keyboard.*

*Group size*
*One to four children.*

## What you need
A small battery keyboard or a small keyboard with transformer, lead and plugs.

## Setting up
Familiarize yourself with the keyboard before trying this activity. CARE! if using a mains lead and adapter. Place the keyboard on the table, ensure that the mains switch and the switch on the keyboard are on.

## What to do
Gather the children around and explain about switching on the keyboard using the on/off switch. Demonstrate some sounds on the keyboard and then ask each child in turn to find and play a sound. Talk about the sounds. When they have all had a turn, show them how they can find different timbres by altering the numbers with a button or voice selector. (Usually the numbers are digital and are seen on a large red or green display screen. Pressing the keypad simply scrolls through the numbers and if the keys are touched they will play a different sound such as trumpet, harp, piano and so on.)

When they have listened to some of the different timbres, ask them in turn to find one that they like. Listen to each child's sound, value it and talk about it.

Next show them how to make a quiet sound and a loud sound by operating the volume control. Ask one child to play the notes on the keyboard and help another to operate the volume control. Encourage the children to explore until they become confident at finding and making sounds.

### Questions to ask
Can you show me how to switch the keyboard on and off? Can you play a sound for us to listen to? Can you find some different sounds? (By using the number selection.) How can we make a quiet/loud sound? (By using the volume control.) Which sound do you like? (Later) Can you find the sound that you liked again?

### For younger children
Encourage younger children to explore and make different sounds on the keyboard without proceeding to the volume control and voice selection operations.

### For older children
Let them work in pairs to select different instrument voices on the keyboard and explore the loud/quiet volume control.

**Follow-up activities**
● Use photocopiable page 64: talk about the pictures, encouraging the children to move around like the person or animal in the picture and to make up appropriate sounds for them.
● Use the keyboard as an adult resource in story time, adding sounds where appropriate and asking children to tell you about the sounds afterwards.
● Repeat the story later and ask individual children to come out and either find the sound which you chose for a particular point in the story or to make their own suggestions.

# MUSICAL FIREWORKS

**Learning objective**
*To create vocal and instrumental firework sounds.*

**Group size**
*Four to six children.*

## What you need
Pictures of fireworks exploding, in different colours and shapes, selection of instruments and sound sources (shakers, castanets, whistles) and a keyboard (optional), tape recorder, blank tape, recording of firework sounds.

## Setting up
Mount the pictures at child height, either on the wall or on a board placed on the floor. Lay out the instruments in a small group with enough space for the children to sit around them.

## What to do
Do the firework activity, page 44, before this activity.

Look at the firework pictures with the children and remind them of the movements which they explored in the previous activity. Talk about what they did: whirling around for a Catherine wheel, shooting upwards for a rocket, cascading outwards with their arms for 'golden rain'. Encourage them to talk about the colours and sounds.

If you have some tape recorded firework sounds, listen to them and talk about them. Taking each picture in turn, encourage the children to suggest and make sounds with their voices or instruments for each one. Listen to each child's contribution and praise their efforts. Make up some sounds yourself and ask them to join in with you, if they are reticent. If any child appears worried by the louder sounds, concentrate on the sounds for a smaller, quieter firework.

When they have made and tried out a number of suggestions, explain that you are going to tape record their sounds. Label the tape as 'firework music'. Encourage children to listen to it again during exploration times.

## Questions to ask
What firework is this in the picture? What sound does it make? Does it crackle, pop, whizz, bang? What sound does it make to begin with? What happens next? (For example a rocket will make a loud 'whooshing' sound to begin with and will then crackle and bang.) Can you make the 'whooshing' sound? (Join in with me!)

## For younger children
Concentrate on thinking of the sounds for one firework, looking at one of the pictures. Let them copy some of your suggestions. Encourage them to experiment and to explore with the instruments.

## For older children
Encourage them to suggest ideas, make sounds together at the same time and record the sounds. Encourage them to think of the sequence of sounds in a firework explosion and to play the sequence.

**Follow-up activities**
● Make pictures of fireworks using, paints, pastels and crayons; mount the work as a display.
● Make a 3D model of a rocket using junk material; suspend it from the ceiling.
● Talk about the safety aspect of fireworks and the care of animals.

# MAGIC SOUND HOOP

*Learning objective*
*To respond to the*
*sounds made by*
*different materials and*
*artefacts.*

*Group size*
*One to two children.*

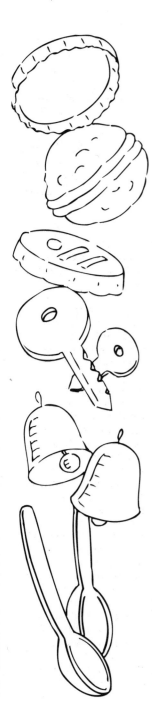

## What you need
A hoop covered in coloured ribbon or paper, objects made from different materials and which make different sounds (choose lightweight objects and aim for variety). Suspend the objects from the hoop using coloured ribbon or cord.

## Setting up
Suspend the hoop in a horizontal plane from a rail or hook, ensuring that the objects can be reached and touched by children. (CARE!). Set this up preferably in a corner so that children of a different height will not walk into it. (Afterwards the hoop can be hung at a much higher level, to be out of reach of all children, or hung vertically from the wall at child height.)

## What to do
Introduce the children to the hoop explaining that there are lots of small sounds hung from it which they are going to explore. Tell them that there is a magic world of sound inside the hoop. Help a child to stand inside and underneath the hoop and encourage him/her to feel the objects and listen to the sounds. Do not intervene too much. Ask few questions and allow the child to respond in his/her own way. You will need to respond in different ways to different children, asking more questions of some than others and allowing some to stand and respond in their own way without asking any questions at all.

## Questions to ask
Questioning should be used judiciously in this activity. At the outset you can draw attention to qualities of the sounds and materials with questions such as: Can you feel this? Is it rough or smooth? Can you make a sound with this one? Can you tell me anything about the sound? Is it rustly, jangly, loud, quiet? Does it make you think of anything? Does it make you feel bouncy, sleepy?

You need to give space and time for individual children to respond in their own way. For many their response will not be a verbal one.

## For younger children
Younger children can be encouraged to explore the sounds and will probably want to touch everything. They will possibly need a shorter time in the hoop and you might be able to help them to concentrate on one or two particular sounds.

## For older children
Older children can be encouraged to play different sounds one after another and might want to tell you what they think of when they are in the hoop.

---

**Follow-up activities**
● Collect other sound sources and suspend them from a small hoop or coat hanger covered in ribbon. These can be hung around the classroom on the walls or suspended from the ceiling.
● Make a small shaker from a thin tube, covered in paint or coloured paper and attach one or two sound sources to the end using materials such as foil bottle tops.
● Lay two hoops flat on the floor. Ask two children to each choose their favourite sound and to sit on the floor inside a hoop with the instrument or sound source. Let them explore the sounds individually, together and then one after the other.

# CHIMING BARS

*Learning objective*
To make up musical patterns.

*Group size*
Two to four children.

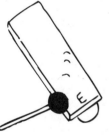

## What you need
Three chime bars for each child (for preference use the notes CDE and GAB, avoid using sharps and flats) and a beater (preferably soft head). A tape recorder and blank tape.

## Setting up
Place the chime bars in groups of three on a table and lay a beater beside each group. Arrange the bars in sequential order for example: CDE and GAB. Ensure that the table height enables children to stand and play the chime bars comfortably, the table should be no higher than their elbows when they are standing up.

## What to do
Explain that the beaters must not be put in their mouths because they are used to play the chime bars and are dangerous if swallowed. (CARE!)

Encourage children to explore and experiment with the sounds to begin with. Help them to use the beaters correctly so that they bounce off the chime bars and let the sound ring. Demonstrate how it sounds with a stiff wrist and the beater not bouncing. Show them the difference when you let the beater bounce with a loose wrist. Ask them to notice the difference in sound.

Next show the children that they can play the bars one after the other. Ask them to copy you. Next ask them to play them one after the other in reverse. Once they can go up and down, explain how you can make the sound jump around, missing out one note.

Encourage the children to explore and make up their own patterns and to hum or sing while they are playing. Listen to each child's pattern in turn and tape record their patterns.

## Questions to ask
Can you hear the beater bouncing? Can you make the beater climb up the steps? Can you make the beater climb back down the steps? Can you make the beater jump and miss out a step? Can you make it jump around?

## For younger children
Start by using the beater with one chime bar and learning how to make it bounce. Help them to control the beater and encourage them to make random patterns on three notes without talking about the steps and jumps.

## For older children
Older children can try out different rhythm patterns using their own names or other words such as fruits or transport (train, car, bicycle). Let them create patterns according to how they say the words so that, for instance, the three syllables of bi/cy/cle should not be equal.

**Follow-up activities**
● Chalk three chime bars on the playground, practise stepping from one to another and jumping backwards and forwards. Hum or sing the 'notes' as you jump or step.
● Encourage the children to join in with sounds for a story after they have heard it a few times. Ask for their suggestions for when they could play certain sounds. For instance snowflakes in a weather story, butterflies in a garden/outdoors story.
● If you have xylophones or glockenspiels, show the children how to slide the beater across a whole row of notes to make a 'glissando'. Encourage the children to make their own sliding sounds.

# MONSTER MUSIC

*Learning objective*
To explore sounds
imaginatively.

*Group size*
One to four children.

## What you need
Pictures of monster animals, children's models of
monsters made from modelling clay, selection
of sound sources and instruments, tape
recorder and a blank tape.

## Setting up
Use a large space for this activity. Place the
instruments in a group on the floor leaving
enough space for the children to gather round in
a circle. Put up the pictures nearby or have them
mounted on boards in front of you. Place the tape
recorder and blank tape near you (CARE!).

## What to do
Talk about the pictures, inviting children's comments on the monsters.
Look at some of the models they have made and observe whether
any of them are like the pictures.

Ask the children to think about a large, loud, scary monster and to
tell you about it. Talk about the loud sounds which a large monster
would make. Ask individual children to imagine the monster and
then encourage them to move around like the monster.

Give each child an instrument and ask them to make loud sounds.
Play some sounds yourself and ask two or three children to move
around while you do so. Think about the sounds made while the
animal walks, runs, calls, cries, eats and sleeps. Value the children's
suggestions. When children have suggested and played a sound, ask
other children if they can copy the sound.

Tape record the monster music, label the tape with the children's
names and place it in a tape rack near to the models and paintings.

## Questions to ask
What can you see in the picture? Is he a real animal or a pretend
animal? Can you show me how the monster moves? Is he quick?
How does it sound when he walks? Can you show me how you think
he walks? Is his mouth big? What sound do you think he makes when
he eats? Do you think he eats very carefully or quietly?

## For younger children
Demonstrate some heavy, loud sounds and ask them to move around
to them. Next, ask them to find some sounds themselves, such as
making loud sounds on a tambour or drum.

## For older children
Older children can control their sounds to produce combinations such
as loud and slow, fast and loud and then play their sounds with
another child.

**Follow-up activities**
● Join together in a
group of three to
five, holding each
other's waists and
move around slowly,
making vocal sounds
for the monster.
● Make a huge
model of a monster
using junk material.
Involve children in
painting parts of the
monster and adding
fantasy 'skin' or 'fur'
from a mixture of soft
and hard materials
such as tissue, wood
shavings, pasta
shapes, wool, string,
shiny Cellophane.
● Make huge foot
prints for the monster
and paint them.
Make a trail on the
floor leading from the
model to outside or
to another area of the
room.
● Listen to 'Atem',
'Circulation of Events'
and 'Wahn' by
Tangerine Dream.
● Move around
imaginatively like
monsters.

# THE THREE BEARS

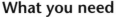

*Learning objective*
*To listen to a piece of*
*recorded music and*
*recognize what is*
*happening in the story.*

*Group size*
*One to eight children.*

## What you need
A recording of 'The Three Bears Fantasy' by Eric Coates, CD player
or tape recorder. Story of 'Goldilocks and The Three Bears'
(Traditional).

## What to do
This activity needs to be done in stages at different times. First
tell the story of 'Goldilocks and the Three Bears' using a story
book with pictures. Question the children and ensure that
they know and understand the story well.

Gather the children around you and explain that you are going to
hear a story about three bears. Explain that today the story is going
to sound different, because they will hear music to tell it. Explain that
they must sit very still and be quiet whilst they listen.

Tell them that they will hear an instrument playing the sounds to
represent 'Who's been sitting in my chair?'. Say the words with the
children and beat the rhythm on a drum. Tell them to listen for it
(track one). The next track depicts Goldilocks setting out into the wood
feeling quite happy and in the third track, we hear Goldilocks arriving
at the house of the three bears and knocking loudly on the door.
Depending on the attention span of the children and how well they
know the story, it should be possible to reach this point.

Wherever you get to in the story, ask the children what happens
next and through questioning reach the end of the story. Build up the
children's attention span gradually. On the next occasion, tell the
start of the story verbally and quite quickly and then play the next
part of the music.

You should eventually play all of the story. Increase the children's
attention by involving four children in role play throughout the part
of the story which you're listening to or by everyone joining in with
the actions, smiling and swaying as Goldilocks goes to the wood,
banging on the door, tasting the porridge and falling asleep.

## Questions to ask
Can you say the words, 'Who's been sitting in my chair?' Listen to the
drum saying those words: can you say them as I beat the drum? Listen
to Goldilocks going off into the wood. Do you think she is happy or
sad? How do you know?

## For younger children
Keep the listening sections very short and explain the story section
beforehand. Ask them to join in with the actions when they can.

## For older children
Older children can role play the story and sequence more of the
actions. By questioning, encourage them to focus more on the music
and to recognize the musical cues for the storyline.

**Follow-up activities**
● Children can role
play the story
without the recorded
music and make up
their own sounds to
fit in with it.
● Draw pictures of
Goldilocks and the
three bears, showing
the relative different
sizes.
● Find some very
high sounds to
represent baby bear
and very low sounds
for daddy bear, using
the keyboard. Use a
battery keyboard and
stand the instrument
vertically (while
holding it) to show
the children more
easily where the high
and low sounds are
positioned.

# GRASSHOPPER

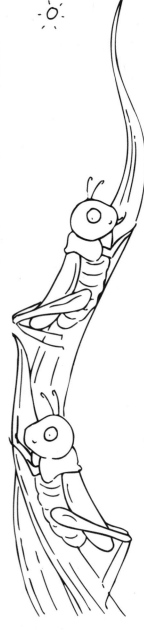

*Learning objective*
To recognize sounds
used by a composer to
represent grasshoppers
and to compose
grasshopper music.

*Group size*
Eight to ten children.

## What you need
A recording of 'The Grasshopper's Dance' by Ernest Bucalossi, pictures
of grasshoppers, selection of guiros (metal and wood) or a rasp, wood
blocks, wood or metal agogos, sheets of fine sandpaper, tape recorder
or CD player. A large space.

## Setting up
Mount the pictures on boards or at child height. Set up the tape
recorder. Place the instruments near to you.

## What to do
Look at the pictures and encourage the children to name the
grasshopper and to tell you about it. Explain that it jumps and that it
makes a sound by rubbing its legs together. Ask the children to rub
their hands together palm to palm and to listen to the sound they
make. Ask one or two children if they could demonstrate how the
grasshopper jumps.

Next tell them that they might be able to hear the sound of a
grasshopper in the music. Ask them to listen carefully for a short
while. Play the music again and encourage the children to join in
when they hear the grasshopper rubbing his legs.

Stop the music and investigate sounds for grasshoppers using the
instruments. Concentrate on the rasping sounds at first with sandpaper
and listen to the sound made by the guiros. Then encourage them to
explore sounds for jumping. Split the children into two groups, one
for rasping sounds and one for jumping sounds.

When they have explored some sounds, listen to 'The Grasshopper's
Dance' again. Children can join in by rubbing their hands, playing a
guiro or sandpaper or by jumping. Play this a few times over a period
of days, letting the children take it in turns to do the movement or
play the instruments.

## Questions to ask
Do you know what this insect is called? What sound/movement does
he make? Can you jump like a grasshopper? Can you brush your
hands together to make a sound? Did you hear the grasshopper in
the music? What instrument could we use for the grasshopper? (Make
smooth and jumping sounds). Which do you think sounds like the
grasshopper? Can you make your sound jump?

## For younger children
Look at the pictures, listen to the music and encourage them to rub
their hands together and to jump with their hands when they hear
the sounds.

## For older children
Encourage them to make up their own sounds and to choose which
they think are best, Encourage them to select and reject sounds.

### Follow-up activities
● Make models and
paintings of
grasshoppers.
● Observe
grasshoppers in the
summer and listen to
and tape record their
sounds.

# PHOTOCOPIABLES

Name _____

Make some music for each picture.

**Name** _____

Cut round the solid lines. Fold on dotted lines. Draw numbers or pictures on the six faces. Place glue on 'stick' sections and stick flaps inside the adjoining face.

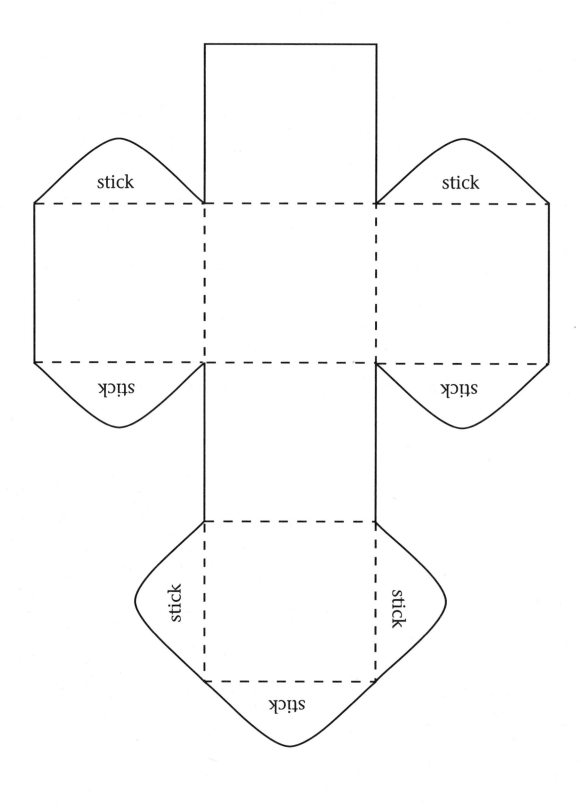

**Name** _____

Make sounds for the pictures. Talk about them and colour them in.

Name _____

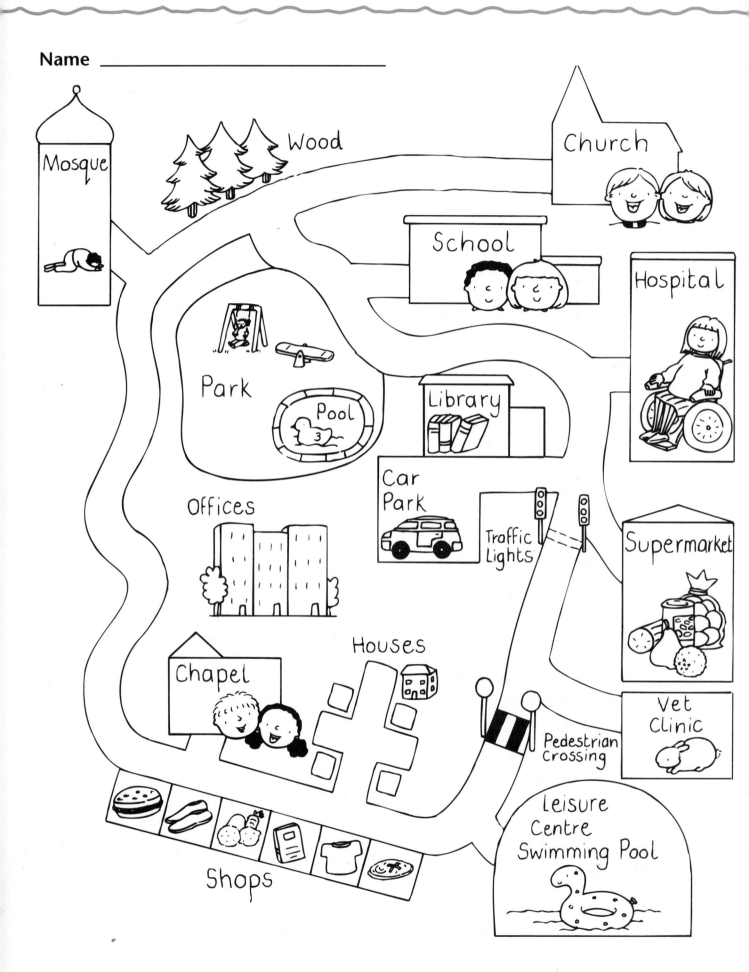

**Name** _____

Can you make sounds for these actions? Do the movements too.
Now colour them in.

**Name** _____

Can you make sounds for each picture? Colour in the pictures.